California HMH SCIENCE DIMENSIONS®

Grade 1

Watch the cover come alive as you match the young animals to their parents.
Download the HMH Science Dimensions AR app available on Android or iOS devices.

This Write-In Book belongs to

_____

Teacher/Room

_____

Consulting Authors

Michael A. DiSpezio
Global Educator
North Falmouth, Massachusetts

Marjorie Frank
Science Writer and Content-Area Reading Specialist
Brooklyn, New York

Michael R. Heithaus, PhD
Dean, College of Arts, Sciences & Education
Professor, Department of Biological Sciences
Florida International University
Miami, Florida

Bernadine Okoro
Access and Equity Consultant
S.T.E.M. Learning Advocate & Consultant
Washington, DC

Cary Sneider, PhD
Associate Research Professor
Portland State University
Portland, Oregon

All images ©Houghton Mifflin Harcourt, Inc., unless otherwise noted

Front cover: ©HMH

Back cover: *chick hatching* ©wisawa222/Shutterstock

Copyright © 2020 by Houghton Mifflin Harcourt Publishing Company

All rights reserved. No part of this work may be reproduced or transmitted in any form or by any means, electronic or mechanical, including photocopying or recording, or by any information storage or retrieval system, without the prior written permission of the copyright owner unless such copying is expressly permitted by federal copyright law. Requests for permission to make copies of any part of the work should be submitted through our Permissions website at https://customercare.hmhco.com/contactus/Permissions.html or mailed to Houghton Mifflin Harcourt Publishing Company, Attn: Intellectual Property Licensing, 9400 Southpark Center Loop, Orlando, Florida 32819-8647.

Printed in the U.S.A.

ISBN 978-1-328-89507-3

7 8 9 10 0877 27 26 25 24 23

4500865925   B C D E F G

If you have received these materials as examination copies free of charge, Houghton Mifflin Harcourt Publishing Company retains title to the materials and they may not be resold. Resale of examination copies is strictly prohibited.

Possession of this publication in print format does not entitle users to convert this publication, or any portion of it, into electronic format.

Program Advisors

Paul D. Asimow, PhD
Eleanor and John R. McMillan Professor of Geology and Geochemistry
California Institute of Technology
Pasadena, California

Eileen Cashman, PhD
Professor
Humboldt State University
Arcata, California

Mark B. Moldwin, PhD
Professor of Space Sciences and Engineering
University of Michigan
Ann Arbor, Michigan

Kelly Y. Neiles, PhD
Assistant Professor of Chemistry
St. Mary's College of Maryland
St. Mary's City, Maryland

Sten Odenwald, PhD
Astronomer
NASA Goddard Spaceflight Center
Greenbelt, Maryland

Bruce W. Schafer
Director of K-12 STEM Collaborations, retired
Oregon University System
Portland, Oregon

Barry A. Van Deman
President and CEO
Museum of Life and Science
Durham, North Carolina

Kim Withers, PhD
Assistant Professor
Texas A&M University-Corpus Christi
Corpus Christi, Texas

Adam D. Woods, PhD
Professor
California State University, Fullerton
Fullerton, California

English Language Development Advisors

Mercy D. Momary
Local District Northwest
Los Angeles, California

Michelle Sullivan
Balboa Elementary
San Diego, California

Classroom Reviewers & Hands-On Activities Advisors

Julie Arreola
Sun Valley Magnet School
Sun Valley, California

Pamela Bluestein
Sycamore Canyon School
Newbury Park, California

Andrea Brown
HLPUSD Science and STEAM TOSA
Hacienda Heights, California

Cynthia Sistek-Chandler, PhD
Associate Professor
National University, Sanford College of Education
San Diego, California

Leslie C. Antosy-Flores
Star View Elementary
Midway City, California

Stephanie Greene
Science Department Chair
Sun Valley Magnet School
Sun Valley, California

Kimberly Ann Huesing
Carlsbad Unified
Carlsbad, California

Rana Mujtaba Khan
Will Rogers High School
Van Nuys, California

George Kwong
Schafer Park Elementary
Hayward, California

Imelda Madrid
Bassett St. Elementary School
Lake Balboa, California

Susana Martinez O'Brien
Diocese of San Diego
San Diego, California

Craig Moss
Mt. Gleason Middle School
Sunland, California

Isabel Souto
Schafer Park Elementary
Hayward, California

Emily R.C.G. Williams
South Pasadena Middle School
South Pasadena, California

Claims, Evidence, and Reasoning ix
Safety in Science xi

Unit 1 • Engineering and Technology 1

Unit Project 3

Language Development 6

Lesson 1 Engineer It • How Do Engineers Use Technology? 8
    Hands-On Activity Engineer It • Solve the Problem 15
    Take It Further—Careers in Science & Engineering • Packaging Engineer 17

Lesson 2 Engineer It • How Can We Solve a Problem? 22
    Hands-On Activity Engineer It • Protect the Legs 31
    Take It Further—People in Science & Engineering • Lynn Conway 33

Unit Performance Task 38
Unit Review 40

Unit 2 • Shadows and Light 43

Unit Project 45

📖 **Language Development** 48

Lesson 1 How Does Light Help Us See? 50
   ✋ **Hands-On Activity** Make Observations in Different Light 55
   Take It Further—People in Science & Engineering •
   Thomas Edison 61

Lesson 2 How Does Light Travel? 66
   ✋ **Hands-On Activity** Test What Happens to Light 75
   Take It Further—Careers in Science & Engineering •
   Camera Engineer 77

Lesson 3 How Do Materials Block Light? 82
   ✋ **Hands-On Activity** Test How Light Passes Through Materials ... 85
   Take It Further—People in Science & Engineering •
   Dr. Patricia Bath 91

Unit Performance Task 96

Unit Review 98

Unit 3 • Plant Parts..................................... 101

Unit Project 103

📖 **Language Development** 106

Lesson 1 Engineer It • What Parts Help Plants Live?............108

✋ **Hands-On Activity** Engineer It • Observe Plants to Design 119
Take It Further—People in Science & Engineering •
Isabella Abbott 121

Lesson 2 How Do Plants Look Like Their Parents? 126

✋ **Hands-On Activity** Grow Carrot Tops................................. 135
Take It Further—Careers in Science & Engineering •
Soil Scientist 137

Unit Performance Task 142

Unit Review 144

Unit 4 • Animal Parts 147

Unit Project 149

Language Development 152

Lesson 1 Engineer It • What Parts Help Animals Live? 154
- Hands-On Activity Engineer It •
  Observe Animals to Design 163
- Take It Further—Careers in Science & Engineering •
  Bioengineer 167

Lesson 2 How Do Animals Look Like Their Parents? 172
- Hands-On Activity Observe Brine Shrimp 177
- Take It Further—People in Science & Engineering •
  Robyn Hannigan 185

Lesson 3 How Do Animals Take Care of Their Young? 190
- Hands-On Activity Compare How Animals Learn 199
- Take It Further—People in Science & Engineering •
  David Mizejewski 201

Unit Performance Task 206

Unit Review 208

Unit 5 • Animal Sounds 211

Unit Project 213

Language Development 216

Lesson 1 What Is Sound? 218

Hands-On Activity Make Something Move with Sound 227
Take It Further—People in Science & Engineering •
José Hernández-Rebollar 229

Lesson 2 Engineer It • How Do Animals Make Sounds? 234

Hands-On Activity Engineer It •
Communicate over Distance 243
Take It Further—Careers in Science & Engineering •
Ethologist 245

Unit Performance Task 250

Unit Review 252

Unit 6 • Objects and Patterns in the Sky .. 255

Unit Project 257

Language Development 260

Lesson 1 What Are Patterns of Objects in the Sky? 262

Hands-On Activity Observe the Pattern of the Sun 267
Take It Further—People in Science & Engineering •
Kalpana Chawla 275

Lesson 2 What Are Patterns of Daylight? 280

Hands-On Activity Observe Patterns of Sunset 289
Take It Further—Careers in Science & Engineering •
Circadian Biologist 291

Unit Performance Task 296

Unit Review 298

Interactive Glossary G1

Index I10

Claims, Evidence, and Reasoning

Make a Claim

A **claim** is a statement you think is true.

You can make a claim about what you observe.

Some solid things sink.

A claim can be made before you investigate.

Both the lemon and lime will sink.

A claim can be made after you investigate.

Lemons float in water, and limes sink.

Claims, Evidence, and Reasoning

Use Evidence and Reasoning

Evidence is information that shows whether or not your claim is true.

Data can be used as evidence. Evidence can come from things you observe or read.

My claim was wrong. A lemon will float, and a lime will sink.

Reasoning tells how or why the evidence supports the claim. You can tell why your claim is true or not. You can tell how you know.

My evidence showed that the lemon floats and the lime sinks. This proves my first claim was not true and my second claim was true.

Safety in Science

Doing science is fun. But a science lab can be dangerous. Know the safety rules and listen to your teacher.

⊘ Do not eat or drink anything.
⊘ Do not touch sharp things.
✓ Wash your hands.
✓ Wear goggles to keep your eyes safe.
✓ Be neat and clean up spills.
✓ Tell your teacher if something breaks.
✓ Show good behavior.

Safety in Science

Circle the pictures where a safety rule is being followed. Place an X on the pictures where a safety rule is not being followed.

Unit 1
Engineering and Technology

Explore Online

You Solve It • Marshmallow Launcher

How can you design something to launch a marshmallow? Go online to explore how to make a marshmallow launcher.

Unit 1 At a Glance

Unit Project 3

Lesson 1
Engineer It • How Do Engineers Use Technology? 8

Lesson 2
Engineer It • How Can We Solve a Problem? 22

Unit Performance Task 38

Unit Review 40

Name _____

Unit Project
Pocket Lock-It

Objects can fall out of pockets. That can be a problem. Plan and conduct an investigation. Design a solution to keep things from falling out of a jacket pocket.

Ask a Question

Record the question.

_____

_____

_____

Materials

Draw and label the materials you will need.

Steps Write the steps you will do.

_____

_____

_____

_____

_____

_____

_____

Data

Record your data.

Analyze Your Results

Look for patterns in your data.

Restate Your Question

Write the question you investigated.

_____

_____

_____

Claims, Evidence, and Reasoning

Make a claim that answers your question.

_____

_____

_____

Review the data. What evidence from the investigation supports your claim?

_____

_____

_____

Discuss your reasoning with a partner.

Unit 1 • Engineering and Technology

Language Development

As you work through the lessons, fill in the chart using definitions and examples.

Word	What it means
engineer	A person who solves problems.
problem	
solution	
technology	
design process	

Example	Words I know that are like it
someone who plans roads	builder, planner

Lesson 1
Engineer It • How Do Engineers Use Technology?

People make things to solve problems.

Explore First

Object Hunt Observe objects in your classroom. Which objects do you think an engineer made? Record your ideas in your Evidence Notebook.

Understand the Problem

Explore Online

Mia uses headphones to listen to music. She keeps them in her pocket.

Can You Explain It?

✏️ What is Mia's problem? How can you understand the problem to solve it?

_____

_____

_____

Lesson 1 • Engineer It • How Do Engineers Use Technology?

What Is an Engineer?

Explore Online

Engineers use science and math to build bridges.

Engineers make cars that do not need gas.

Engineers build rides that are safe.

An **engineer** is a person who uses math and science to solve problems. A **problem** is something that needs to be fixed or made better. Engineers look for solutions. A **solution** is something that fixes a problem.

Engineers name the problem.

Engineers ask questions about the problem. They observe and gather information.

Engineers can solve a problem. First they have to understand the problem.

Lesson 1 • Engineer It • How Do Engineers Use Technology? 11

What do engineers do? Choose all correct answers.

Ⓐ find and solve problems

Ⓑ use math and science

Ⓒ ask questions

Apply What You Know

Evidence Notebook • Act like an engineer. Put headphones in your pocket. Walk around the room for two minutes. What problem happens? Work with a group. Ask questions about the problem. Write down your questions. Then make observations and gather evidence.

_____

_____

_____

What Is Technology?

Explore Online

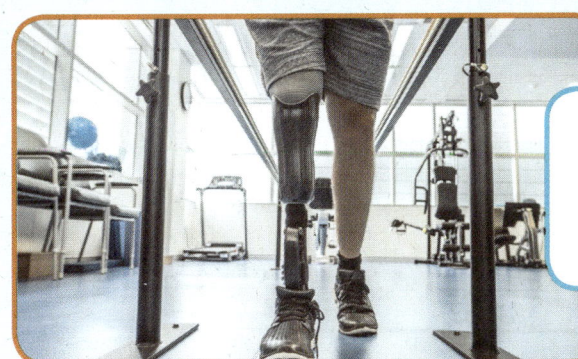

Technology can help someone walk.

Technology can be simple, like a hammer.

Technology is what engineers make to meet needs and solve problems. Technology can even be an idea from observing nature. The idea for planes came from observing birds.

Which objects are technology? Choose all correct answers.

Ⓐ a lamp

Ⓑ a tree

Ⓒ a pencil

Do the Math! • This tally chart shows how children in one class use technology each day.

Classroom Technology	
pencil	|||||
tablet	||||| ||||
cell phone	|||||	

 How many more children use a tablet than a cell phone each day?

_____ more children

Apply What You Know

Read, Write, Share! • **Evidence Notebook** • Find three kinds of technology. How do you know each one is technology? What problems do they solve? Use evidence to answer the questions. Write to explain your answers.

Name_____

Hands-On Activity

Engineer It • Solve the Problem

Explore Online

Materials • headphones • classroom materials

Ask a Question

Test and Record Data

Step 1

Explain the problem. Gather information about the problem.

Step 2

Plan two solutions to the problem.

Lesson 1 • Engineer It • How Do Engineers Use Technology?

Step 3

Use the classroom materials to build your solutions.

Step 4

Share your solutions. Talk about how the shape of each solution solved the problem.

Make a claim that answers your question.

What is your evidence?

Take It Further

Careers in Science & Engineering • Packaging Engineer

Explore more online.
- Palatasa Havea
- Transportation Timeline

Explore Online

What do packaging engineers do? Here's a hint. You see their work on store shelves every day.

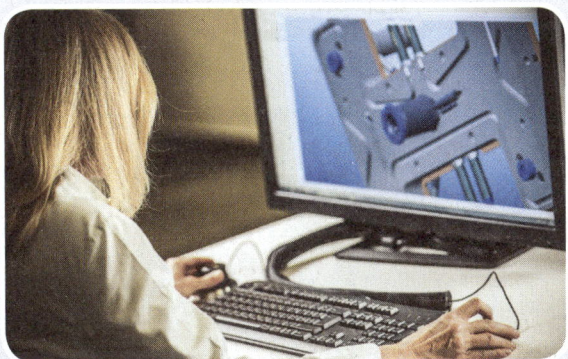

They design packages. They choose materials and decide how the materials will affect the environment.

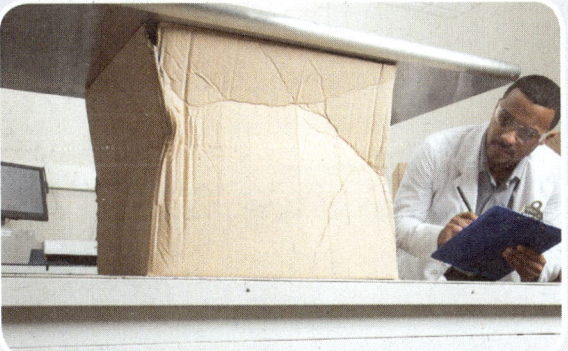

Then they test their ideas. They drop and crush the packages! They make sure what is inside is protected.

A factory builds the final packages.

✏️ Draw a line to match each object with the best way to package it.

Lesson Check

Name _____

Can You Explain It?

✏️ What is Mia's problem? How can you understand the problem to solve it?

Be sure to

- Name Mia's problem.
- Tell the steps needed to understand the problem to solve it.

_____

_____

_____

_____

Lesson 1 • Engineer It • How Do Engineers Use Technology?

Self Check

1. What does an engineer do first?

    Ⓐ gather information about a problem

    Ⓑ find a solution to a problem

    Ⓒ name a problem

2. Which objects are examples of technology? Circle all correct answers.

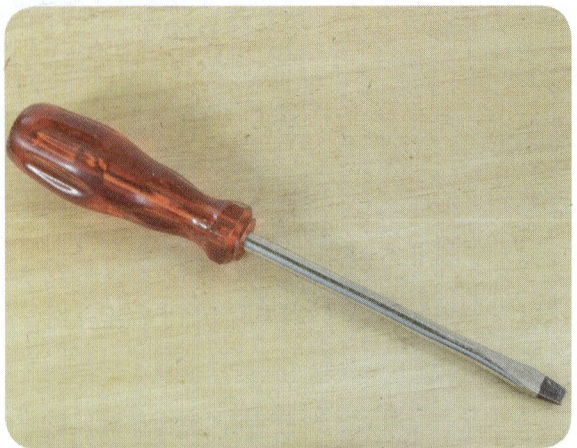

3. Which is a problem technology could solve?

   Ⓐ Theo's backpack straps are hard to wear.

   Ⓑ Maya lost a letter in her house.

   Ⓒ Hector does not agree with his sister.

4. What does the picture show?

   Ⓐ an engineer

   Ⓑ technology

   Ⓒ a problem

5. How do engineers understand a problem? Choose all correct answers.

   Ⓐ They ask questions.

   Ⓑ They observe things.

   Ⓒ They gather information.

Lesson 2
Engineer It • How Can We Solve a Problem?

Engineers solve big and small problems.

Explore First

Leash Materials Test materials to use for a dog leash. Decide which material would be best to use. Explain why you chose your material.

The Pulling Dog Problem

Explore Online

Max's dog keeps pulling on its leash.

Can You Solve It?

✏️ What steps would you take to solve the problem of a dog pulling during a walk?

_____

_____

_____

Lesson 2 • Engineer It • How Can We Solve a Problem?

Step 1–Define a Problem

Explore Online

A Design Process

1. Define a Problem
2. Plan and Build
3. Test and Improve
4. Redesign
5. Communicate

How can we solve problems? One way to solve problems is to follow a design process. A **design process** is a plan with steps that helps engineers find good solutions.

The treats for Tara's dog keep crumbling when she puts them in her pocket. It's messy! This is a problem. She needs to find a way to protect the treats.

Tara defines her problem. She gathers information about the problem.

Explore Online

What is Step 1 of a design process?

_____

Apply What You Know

Define a problem in your classroom. Make observations and gather information about the problem. Talk with others about the problem. Tell what you know about it.

Step 2–Plan and Build

Explore Online

What does Tara do next? She thinks of an idea for two solutions that will hold and protect the treats. She chooses her materials and builds the solutions.

✏️ You want to plan a solution. What is the first thing you should do?

_____

Apply What You Know

Think about the classroom problem you found. Think of an idea for two solutions. Make models of your solutions. Then choose materials and build your solutions. Follow your models.

Step 3–Test and Improve

Explore Online

Tara tests her solutions. They both protect the treats. But the bag is hard to use, and the long paper roll is tricky to tip over. Can she make either of her solutions better?

✏️ What do you do after you build your solutions?

Apply What You Know

Evidence Notebook • Test your solutions for solving the classroom problem. Which one works best? Use evidence to explain. How would you improve the solution?

Step 4–Redesign

Tara decides to redesign her paper towel roll solution. She thinks a shorter roll will work better, so she cuts it in half. Then she tests the solution again. It works!

Explore Online

✏️ What happens at Step 4 of a design process?

_____

_____

Apply What You Know

Evidence Notebook • Now redesign your solution for the classroom problem. Test the solution. Does the new solution work better? Use evidence to tell how you know.

Step 5–Communicate

Explore Online

Tara draws her final solution and takes a picture of her drawing. You can draw, take photos, or write notes to tell about a solution. Why is this step important? People may want to use your idea. They may try to make it better.

How can you communicate the solution to a problem? Choose all correct answers.

Ⓐ Make drawings.

Ⓑ Take photos.

Ⓒ Write notes.

Do the Math! • Brooke builds two solutions to stop her cat from scratching a chair. She tests Solution 1 three times. She tests Solution 2 six times. Add tally marks to the chart to show how many times Tara tests Solution 2.

Number of Times Tested	
Solution 1	|||
Solution 2	

Apply What You Know

You found a solution to your classroom problem. Now tell others about it. Draw a picture of the solution. Write notes to tell what you did. Take some photographs.

Name_____

Hands-On Activity
Engineer It • Protect the Legs!

Explore Online

Materials • a fork • classroom materials
• a small chair

Ask a Question

_____

Test and Record Data

Step 1

Define the problem.

_____

_____

Step 2

Plan two solutions. Choose the materials you will use.

Step 3

Build your solutions. Follow your plan.

Lesson 2 • Engineer It • How Can We Solve a Problem?

Step 4

Test your solutions. Look for ways to improve your solutions.

Step 5

Think of a way you could redesign your solutions. Share your solutions.

Make a claim that answers your question.

What is your evidence?

Take It Further
People in Science & Engineering •
Lynn Conway

Explore more online.
- Agricultural Engineer
- Solve a Paw-blem

Explore Online

Lynn Conway is an engineer. She designed ways to make computers work faster and better. She wrote a book about computers. The book has been used in many schools to teach other engineers. Conway also taught at the University of Michigan.

 **Read, Write, Share!**

Work with a partner. Look at pictures of computers. How has the way computers look changed? Make a timeline to show how they have changed.

▭▶ Draw your timeline.

Then use connecting words like **then** and **after that** to explain how computers changed. Why do you think they changed?

_____

_____

_____

_____

Lesson Check

Name _____

Explore Online

Can You Solve It?

✏️ What steps would you take to solve the problem of a dog pulling during a walk? Be sure to
- Name the steps in a design process.
- Tell how you would use the steps to solve the problem.

_____
_____
_____
_____
_____

Self Check

1. How do you understand a problem in Step 1 of a design process? Choose all correct answers.

    Ⓐ Ask questions

    Ⓑ Make observations

    Ⓒ Gather information

2. Which step of a design process does the picture show?

    Ⓐ Define a Problem

    Ⓑ Plan and Build

    Ⓒ Communicate

3. Gabriel uses a design process to build a back scratcher. He tests the back scratcher. It is not long enough. What should he do next?

    Ⓐ He should throw out the back scratcher.

    Ⓑ He should communicate his solution.

    Ⓒ He should find ways to improve it.

4. Kim builds a clay boat. The boat needs to be strong enough to hold a few pennies. How will Kim know her boat works?

Ⓐ She should test if the boat floats.

Ⓑ She should test if the pennies float.

Ⓒ She should test if the water is high enough.

5. Juan builds a shelf for his books. The shelf keeps falling over. He finds new materials and rebuilds it. What problem is he solving?

Ⓐ Juan's books are not light enough.

Ⓑ Juan's shelf is not strong enough.

Ⓒ Juan does not have enough books.

Unit Performance Task
Engineer It • Build a House

Materials
- cardboard
- paper
- craft sticks
- tape
- scissors
- fan or blow dryer
- other classroom materials

STEPS

Step 1

Define a Problem You want to build a house that can not be blown down by wind.

Step 2

Plan and Build Plan at least two solutions. Think about the materials you will need. Build your solutions.

Step 3

Test and Improve Test your solutions. How can you improve your solutions?

Step 4

Redesign Make changes to the materials or how you put the materials together. Test your new solutions.

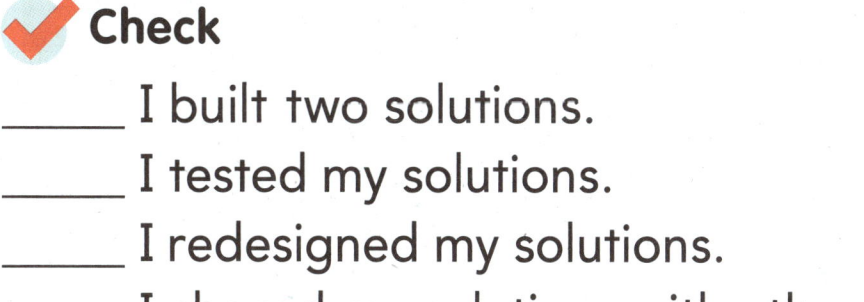

Step 5

Communicate Share your solutions. Explain which materials you used and why you chose them. Use evidence to tell how your solutions solve the problem.

✔ **Check**

_____ I built two solutions.

_____ I tested my solutions.

_____ I redesigned my solutions.

_____ I shared my solutions with others.

Unit Review

Name _____

1. What does an engineer do? Choose all correct answers.
   - Ⓐ uses math and science to solve problems
   - Ⓑ follows a design process
   - Ⓒ makes new technology

2. What is the last thing an engineer does to solve a problem?
   - Ⓐ gather information
   - Ⓑ define the problem
   - Ⓒ build a solution

3. Which objects in the picture are examples of technology? Choose all correct answers.
   - Ⓐ the fishing pole
   - Ⓑ the dock
   - Ⓒ the lake

4. Aman is learning to ride a bike. What technology solves the problem of him falling over?
   - Ⓐ a helmet
   - Ⓑ sneakers
   - Ⓒ training wheels

5. Which problem can Derek solve with technology?
   Ⓐ Derek can not find a piece of paper.
   Ⓑ Derek has a flat tire on his bike.
   Ⓒ Derek can not make up his mind about what snack he wants.

6. Which technology can help solve each problem? Draw a line to match each problem to the technology that can help solve it.

Unit 1 • Review

7. Which is **true** about problems?
   Ⓐ Problems only have one solution.
   Ⓑ Problems can have many solutions.
   Ⓒ Problems can only be solved by engineers.

8. Camila finds a problem. She asks questions, makes observations, and gathers data. What should she do next?
   Ⓐ plan and build
   Ⓑ test and improve
   Ⓒ redesign

9. What step of a design process does the picture show?
   Ⓐ Define a Problem
   Ⓑ Communicate
   Ⓒ Test and Improve

10. Which are ways to communicate a solution? Choose all correct answers.
    Ⓐ Take photos or draw pictures.
    Ⓑ Write notes to tell about it.
    Ⓒ Ask questions and make observations.

Unit 2
Shadows and Light

Explore Online

You Solve It • Message Projector
How can you use light to send a message? Go online to explore how to make a message projector.

Unit 2 At a Glance

Unit Project 45

Lesson 1
How Does Light Help Us See? 50

Lesson 2
How Does Light Travel? 66

Lesson 3
How Do Materials Block Light? 82

Unit Performance Task 96

Unit Review 98

Name _____

Unit Project
Make a Rainbow

You can make a rainbow. Plan and conduct an investigation to make a rainbow.

Ask a Question
Record the question.

_____

_____

_____

Materials
- water • a drinking glass • white paper • bright light

Draw how you could use these materials to make a rainbow.

Steps Write the steps you will do to make a rainbow.

_____

_____

_____

_____

_____

_____

Data

Record your data.

Analyze Your Results

Look for patterns in your data.

Restate Your Question

Write the question you investigated.

_____

_____

_____

Claims, Evidence, and Reasoning

Make a claim that answers your question.

_____

_____

_____

Review the data. What evidence from the investigation supports your claim?

_____

_____

_____

Discuss your reasoning with a partner.

 Language Development

As you work through the lessons, fill in the chart using definitions and examples.

Word	What it means
light	Energy that lets you see.
reflect	
shadow	

Example	Words I know that are like it
sunlight	shine, glow

Lesson 1: How Does Light Help Us See?

Light helps you see things.

 **Explore First**

Lights, Camera Observe a picture that has been taken in a room with little light. Observe a picture that has been taken in a room with a lot of light. Compare what you can see in each picture.

Light in Darkness

Explore Online

It is nighttime. The sky is dark. But you can see fireworks in a dark sky.

Can You Explain It?

How can you see fireworks in a dark sky?

_____

_____

_____

All About Light

Explore Online

The cave is dark. The lamp shines light inside it. This helps a cave explorer see the walls and objects.

Lights in a stadium help players see.

How can you see objects in dark places? You can see objects if light shines on them. Light from lamps helps people see. **Light** is energy that lets you see.

When can you see objects in dark places?

Ⓐ all the time

Ⓑ if you look carefully

Ⓒ when light shines on them

Do the Math! • Emma sees it get daylight. Her clock shows the time. What time does it get daylight?

Ⓐ 6:00

Ⓑ 12:00

Ⓒ 12:30

bright light | some light | low light

The amount of light affects how much you can see. You can see a lot in a room with bright light. You see less when there is only some light. You see very little in low light.

Apply What You Know

Read, Write, Share! • How can you see objects in a dark room? Think about the answer. Turn on a flashlight in a dark classroom. Make observations. Talk with your classmates about your ideas. Listen to your classmates. Ask and answer questions.

Name_____

Hands-On Activity
Make Observations in Different Light

Explore Online

Materials • drawing paper • a pencil

Ask a Question

_____

Test and Record Data

Step 1

Observe your classroom when there is a lot of light. How well can you see objects and details? Record your observations.

_____

_____

Step 2

Now observe the same room when it has only some light. How well can you see the same objects and details? Record your observations.

_____

Lesson 1 • How Does Light Help Us See?

Step 3

Finally, observe the room with very little light. What has changed? Record your observations.

_____

_____

Step 4

Talk about your observations. What caused objects to look different?

Make a claim that answers your question.	**What is your evidence?**

See in the Dark

Explore Online

A campfire gives off its own light. You can see it in the dark.

A glow stick gives off its own light. You can see it in the dark.

You can see an object in the dark if you shine light on it. You can also see an object in the dark if it gives off its own light.

Lesson 1 • How Does Light Help Us See?

✏️ Circle the object you could see best in a dark room.

58

You can not see much inside this dark cave. No objects inside give off their own light.

Explore Online

A spotlight lights up the cave. It shines on rocks and other objects. Then you can see them.

You can not see an object that does not give off light. You can not see an object that has no light shining on it.

Lesson 1 • How Does Light Help Us See?

A hiker can not see a rock in a dark cave. Why not? Choose all correct answers.

Ⓐ The rock is darker than the cave.

Ⓑ There is no light shining on the rock.

Ⓒ The rock does not give off light.

Apply What You Know

Evidence Notebook • Work with a small group. Make your classroom dark. Think about this question, How can you see some objects in the dark? Together, design a simple test to answer the question. Make observations. Use evidence to answer the question.

_____
_____
_____
_____

Take It Further

People in Science & Engineering •
Thomas Edison

Explore more online.
- Laser Engineer
- Animals That Glow

Explore Online

Thomas Edison made many important solutions. He did experiments even when he was a young boy. Edison had hearing problems for most of his life. He said not being able to hear helped him concentrate on his experiments.

early lamp

Edison also built switches and wires that made lights work.

One of Edison's most important solutions was the light bulb. He made one of the first light bulbs. Light bulbs need electricity to work. Edison helped bring electricity to people's homes.

 Read, Write, Share!

How do you think electricity changed the way people lived? Present your ideas to classmates. Listen as other classmates present their ideas.

Lesson Check

Name _____

Explore Online

Can You Explain It?

✏️ How can you see fireworks in a dark sky?

Be sure to
- Explain when you can see objects in the dark.

_____
_____
_____
_____

Self Check

1. When can you see an object? Choose all correct answers.

    Ⓐ when it is dark

    Ⓑ when the object gives off light

    Ⓒ when light shines on the object

2. How could you test if an object gives off its own light?

    Ⓐ Put it under a lamp.

    Ⓑ Try to see it in the dark.

    Ⓒ Shine a flashlight on it.

3. Which objects give off their own light? Choose all correct answers.

    Ⓐ the sun

    Ⓑ glow sticks

    Ⓒ fires

4. You can see a few objects in this living room. Tell the cause.

   Ⓐ There are many lamps in the room

   Ⓑ There are no lamps in the room.

   Ⓒ There is one lamp in the room.

5. The campers see the fire. What causes them to see it?

   Ⓐ A light shines on the fire.

   Ⓑ The space around the fire is dark.

   Ⓒ The fire gives off its own light.

Lesson 1 • How Does Light Help Us See?

Lesson 2 — How Does Light Travel?

Light can move from one place to another.

 **Explore First**

Light Bounce What happens to light when it hits an object? Shine light on different objects. Observe. Record what happens to the light in your Evidence Notebook.

Light in Your Eyes

Explore Online

The sun's light shines right in Manu's eyes. Light in your eyes can be a problem.

Can You Solve It?

✏️ How could you point light away from your eyes?

_____

_____

_____

Straight On

Explore Online

The light travels through the water in the tank. It travels in a straight line.

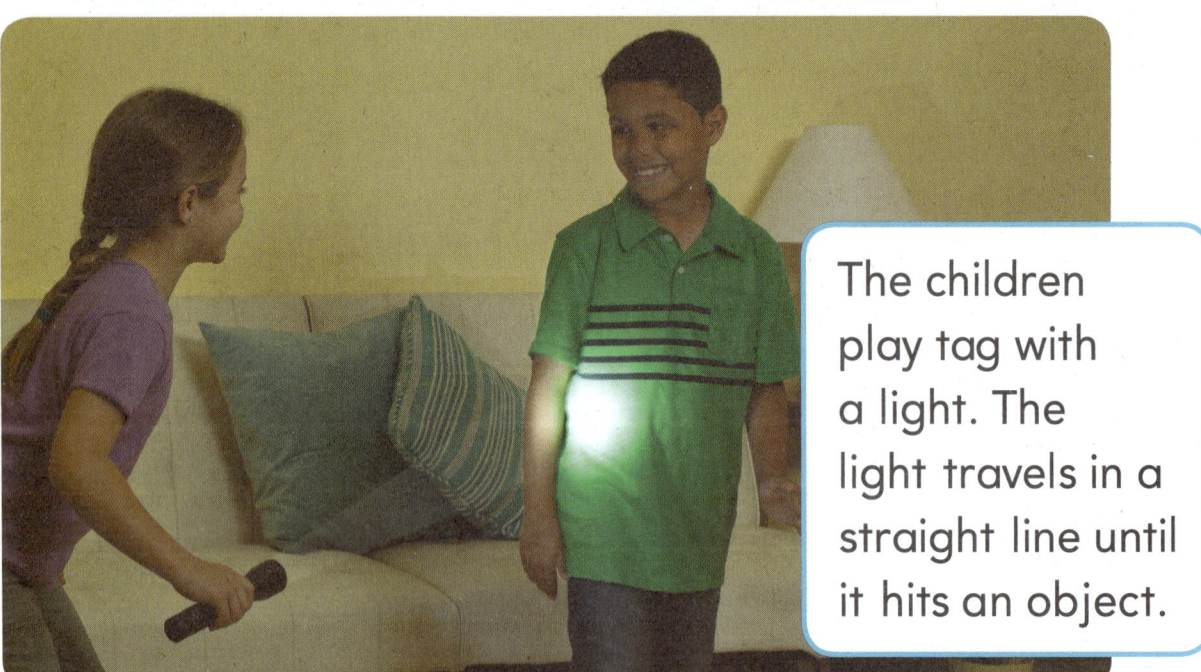

The children play tag with a light. The light travels in a straight line until it hits an object.

Light travels in a straight line until it hits an object.

The light hits the glass. All the light passes through the glass.

The light hits the cardboard. Light is taken in by the cardboard.

The light hits the foil. The light bounces back.

When light hits an object, different things may happen. The light can pass through, be taken in, or bounce back.

Lesson 2 • How Does Light Travel?

✏️ What happens to light when it hits each object? Draw a line to match each picture to the correct label.

The light passes through.

The light is taken in.

The light bounces back.

What does the light in the water tank show about light?

Ⓐ Light does not travel.

Ⓑ Light travels in a straight line.

Ⓒ Light never hits objects.

Apply What You Know

Evidence Notebook • Work with a group. Answer the question, How can we show that light travels in a straight line? Use cards and a flashlight. Give your opinion about how to set up the cards and flashlight. Listen to the opinions of your classmates. Use evidence to answer the question.

Lesson 2 • How Does Light Travel?

A New Direction

Explore Online

Look at the pictures to explore how surfaces can reflect light.

Light hits the mirror. It reflects off the mirror and moves in a new direction.

Smooth and shiny surfaces can reflect light. **Reflect** means to bounce back from a surface.

When the mirror moves, the light moves in a different direction.

Light can move in a new direction when it hits a smooth, shiny surface.

 Draw a surface that can reflect light.

Lesson 2 • How Does Light Travel?

Do the Math! • A beam of light travels 5 feet. A mirror reflects it. The light travels 6 feet more. Then it bounces off a metal door and travels 2 feet more. How many feet does the light travel in all?

Ⓐ 11 feet

Ⓑ 13 feet

Ⓒ 15 feet

 Apply What You Know

Evidence Notebook • Can you reflect light so it hits a spot you want? Work with a partner. Use a flashlight and three small mirrors to make light hit a spot you want. Then talk with your classmates. Collect evidence. Write and draw in your Evidence Notebook. Use evidence to explain if your test worked.

Name_____

Hands-On Activity
Test What Happens to Light

Explore Online

Materials • a flashlight   • a mirror
• a metal spoon   • tin foil   • tin pan

Ask a Question

_____

Test and Record Data

Step 1

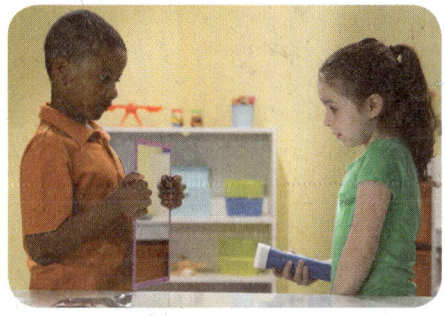

Plan a way to test how smooth, shiny surfaces affect a beam of light. Write your plan.

Step 2

Use the materials to do your test. Record what happens.

Lesson 2 • How Does Light Travel?   75

Step 3

Explain what happened to the beam of light. Identify cause and effect.

Cause	Effect

Make a claim that answers your question.

What is your evidence?

Take It Further
Careers in Science & Engineering •
Camera Engineer

Explore more online.
Art with Light

Explore Online

camera engineer

What do camera engineers do? They help design and build cameras for photos, movies, and videos. They may make large cameras for movies. They may make small cameras that go inside cell phones.

movie camera

cell phone camera

Read, Write, Share!

What would you like to ask a camera engineer? Write at least two questions. Work with a partner to answer your questions. Write to explain what you found. Share what you learned with others.

Lesson Check

Name _____

Can You Solve It?

✏️ How could you point light away from your eyes?

Be sure to

- Explain what kind of surface can point light in a new direction.
- Describe how the surface points light in a new direction.

_____

_____

_____

_____

Lesson 2 • How Does Light Travel?

Self Check

1. Ted thinks that smooth, shiny surfaces reflect light. How could he use a flashlight to test his idea?

   Ⓐ He could aim the light at a wood door.

   Ⓑ He could turn the flashlight on and off to send a message.

   Ⓒ He could observe what happens when light shines at a mirror.

2. What happens to light when it hits each material? Draw a line to match each picture to the words that tell what happens.

Light is taken in.   Light reflects.   Light passes through.

3. Anna wants to plan an investigation to observe if light travels in a straight line. What should she do in her investigation?

　Ⓐ She should shine a flashlight in a dark room.

　Ⓑ She should observe a piece of cardboard in a room with a lot of light.

　Ⓒ She should observe a piece of tin foil in a room with little light.

4. What happens to light when it hits a smooth, shiny piece of foil?

　Ⓐ It will be taken in.

　Ⓑ It will pass through.

　Ⓒ It will be reflected.

5. Which picture shows an example of light being taken in by an object? Circle the picture.

Lesson 2 • How Does Light Travel?

Lesson 3: How Do Materials Block Light?

Materials block light in different ways.

Explore First

Shadow Walk Look around your school on a sunny day. Observe shadows. What causes the shadows? Why are they different shapes? Record your ideas.

Block the Light

Explore Online

This puppet show is in a dark room. Even though it is dark, you can see different shapes.

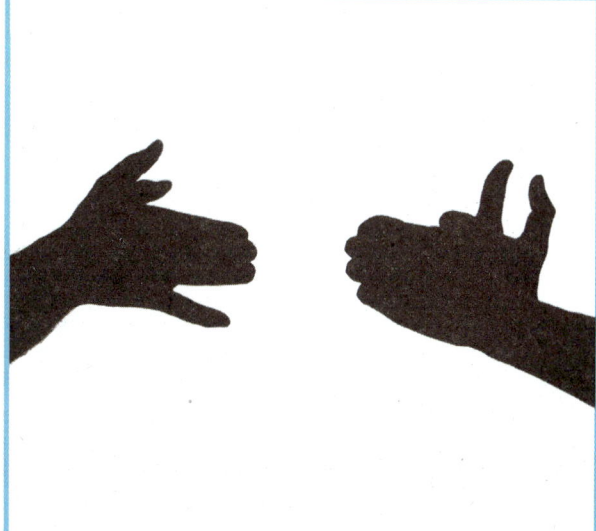

Can You Explain It?

✏️ How does the artist make the shapes?

_____

_____

_____

How Much Light?

Explore Online

No light can pass through wood.

Some light can pass through waxed paper.

All light can pass through clear glass.

Different amounts of light can pass through different materials.

84

Name_____

Hands-On Activity

Test How Light Passes Through Materials

Explore Online

Materials
- a flashlight
- clear plastic
- frosted plastic
- plywood

Ask a Question

_____

Test and Record Data

Step 1

Turn on the flashlight. Shine light through the clear plastic. Observe how much light passes through the plastic.

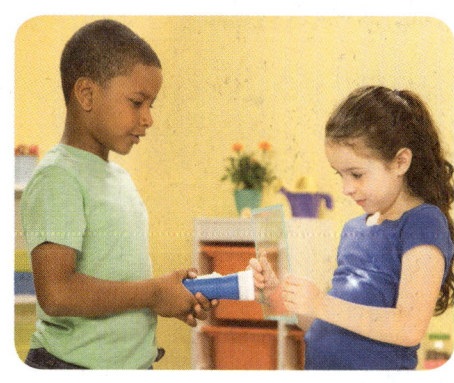

Step 2

Test the rest of the materials. How much light passes through each material? How do you know?

Lesson 3 • How Do Materials Block Light?

85

Step 3

Explain why different materials allow different amounts of light to pass through. Identify cause and effect.

Make a claim that answers your question.

What is your evidence?

How much light passes through a clear glass bowl? Circle the correct answer.

all light

some light

no light

Apply What You Know

Do the Math! • Explore your classroom. Make lists of objects that let all light pass through, some light pass through, and no light pass through. Count and write how many objects are in each group.

All Light	Some Light	No Light
_____	_____	_____

Shadows

Explore Online

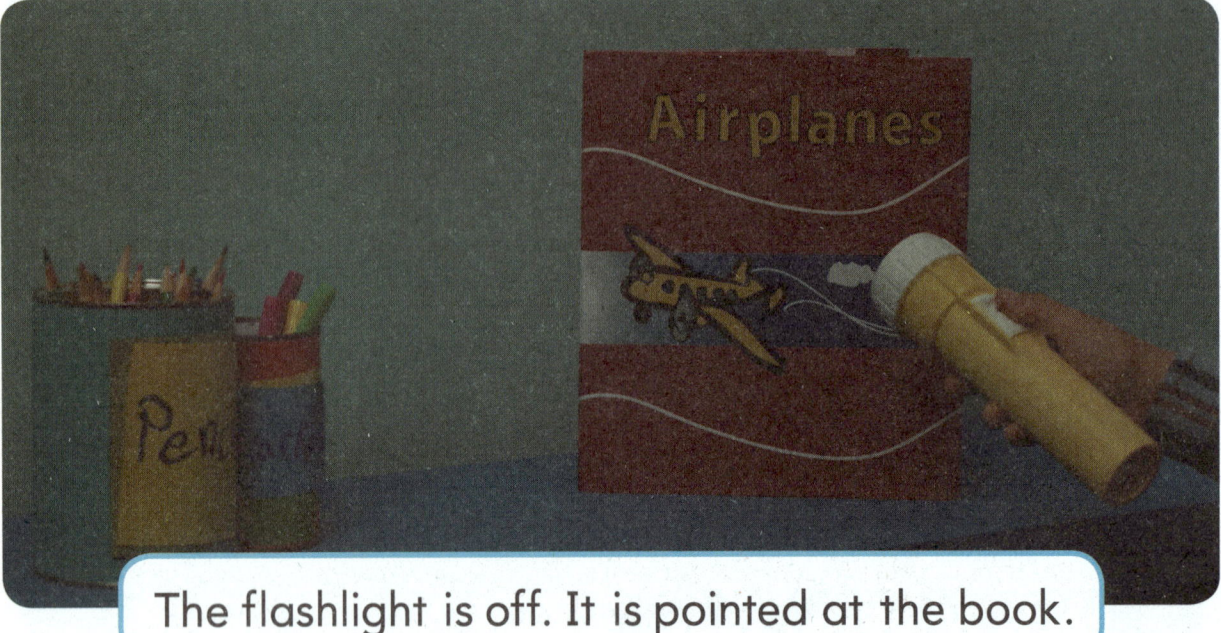

The flashlight is off. It is pointed at the book.

The flashlight is on. The book blocks the light and makes a shadow.

A **shadow** is a dark spot made when an object blocks light. The light does not pass through the object.

Explore Online

The size of a shadow changes when the light shining on the object moves.

Lesson 3 • How Do Materials Block Light?

How will a book's shadow change if light moves closer to the book?

Ⓐ It will get smaller.

Ⓑ It will get bigger.

Ⓒ It will stay the same size.

 Apply What You Know

Evidence Notebook • Work with a group. How does the shape of an object affect its shadow? Design a test using paper and light to answer the question. Talk about your ideas using the words **light** and **shadow**. Do your test. Gather evidence. Use evidence to answer the question.

Take It Further
People in Science & Engineering •
Dr. Patricia Bath

> **Explore more online.**
> - Eye Doctor
> - Make a Sundial

Explore Online

Dr. Patricia Bath has helped people who lost their eyesight. She designed a machine that uses lasers to fix eye problems. Dr. Bath has helped teach people all over the world about eyesight.

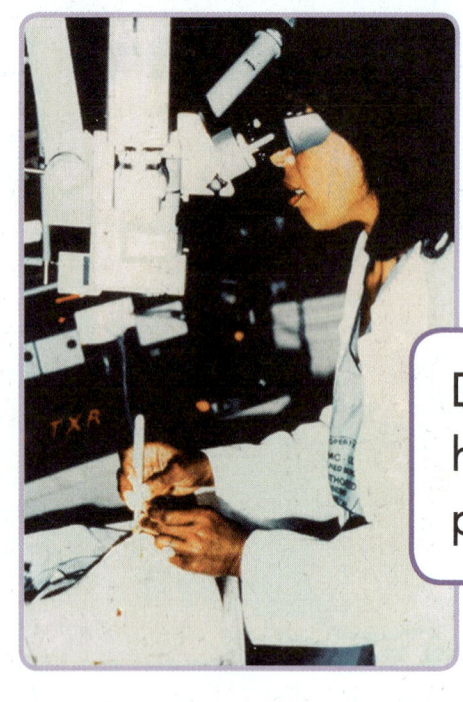

Dr. Bath's machine has helped many people to see again.

 Read, Write, Share!

Dr. Bath taught people about how to take care of their eyesight. What do you want to know about how to take care of your eyesight? Work with a partner. Ask and answer questions.

✏️ Write your questions.

_____
_____
_____

Lesson Check

Name _____

Explore Online

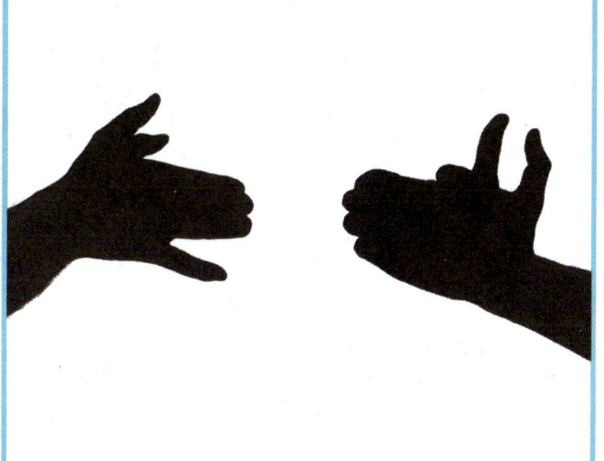

Can You Explain It?

✏️ How does the artist make the shapes?

Be sure to
- Explain that different amounts of light can pass through different materials.
- Explain how shadows are made.

_____
_____
_____
_____

Self Check

1. Which cup allows the most light to pass through? Circle the cup.

2. How much light passes through each object? Match the object to the words that describe it.

| No light passes through. | All light passes through. | Some light passes through. |

3. Eli thinks that all objects block all light. How can he test his idea?

   Ⓐ He can make a shadow on a wall.

   Ⓑ He can move a light closer to an object.

   Ⓒ He can shine light on different objects.

4. Where is the shadow in this picture? Circle it to show your answer.

5. You want to plan an investigation to show how the size of shadows can change. How should you use a flashlight to make a shadow of your hand smaller?

   Ⓐ Keep the flashlight in the same place.

   Ⓑ Move the flashlight closer to your hand.

   Ⓒ Move the flashlight farther from your hand.

Lesson 3 • How Do Materials Block Light?

# Unit Performance Task
Observe Reflections

Materials
- mirror
- masking tape
- paper

STEPS

Step 1

Attach the mirror to the wall. Look into the mirror. You see your reflection because light bounces off your face.

Step 2

Stand to the side and look in the mirror. What parts of the room do you see? Write or draw your observations.

Step 3

Work with a partner to cover the mirror. Think about where you each need to stand to see each other in the mirror. Mark those places with tape.

Step 4

Take the paper off the mirror. Then stand on the tape. Can you see your partner? If not, try again. Write or draw to record your observations.

Step 5

Compare your results with others. Talk about how light traveled from your face and bounced off the mirror so your partner could see it.

✔ Check

_____ I observed my reflection in the mirror.
_____ I worked with a partner to guess where to stand.
_____ I recorded my observations.
_____ I compared my results with others.

Unit Review

Name _____

1. In which room could you see the most objects?
   - Ⓐ a room with bright light
   - Ⓑ a room with some light
   - Ⓒ a room with low light

2. Why can you see fireworks in the night sky?
   - Ⓐ The sky around the fireworks is dark.
   - Ⓑ Fireworks give off their own light.
   - Ⓒ Light shines on the fireworks.

3. What could you do to make the objects in this room easier to see?
   - Ⓐ Turn on more lamps.
   - Ⓑ Turn off all lamps.
   - Ⓒ Make the light lower.

4. How much light can pass through each window? Match each window to the words that describe it.

| No light passes through. | All light passes through. | Some light passes through. |

5. What causes a shadow?
   Ⓐ An object blocks light.
   Ⓑ An object gives off its own light.
   Ⓒ Light shines on an object.

6. You want to plan an investigation to show how your shadow on a wall can be made bigger. You have a lamp that is turned on. What should you do?
   Ⓐ Walk closer to the lamp.
   Ⓑ Step away from the lamp.
   Ⓒ Jump up and down in the same spot.

7. Which sentences are true about the way light travels? Choose all correct answers.
   Ⓐ Light can move around objects.
   Ⓑ Light travels in a straight line until it hits an object.
   Ⓒ Light can reflect off an object.

8. Which objects could you use to reflect light? Choose all correct answers.
   Ⓐ a piece of foil
   Ⓑ a wooden spoon
   Ⓒ a mirror

9. Brad tests what happens when he places a metal spoon in the path of a beam of light. What will he most likely see?
   Ⓐ The light will pass through the spoon.
   Ⓑ The spoon will take in all the light.
   Ⓒ The light will reflect off the spoon.

10. What is the effect of shining a light on a piece of cardboard?
    Ⓐ Light is taken in by the cardboard.
    Ⓑ Light passes through the cardboard.
    Ⓒ Light bounces back from the cardboard.

Unit 3
Plant Parts

Explore Online

You Solve It • Watch Us Grow

How do young plants and adult plants look alike and different? Go online to explore young plants and adult plants.

Unit 3 At a Glance

Unit Project......................... 103

Lesson 1
Engineer It • What Parts Help Plants Live?................ 108

Lesson 2
How Do Plants Look Like Their Parents?.................... 126

Unit Performance Task......... 142

Unit Review 144

Name _____

Unit Project
Explore Plant Parts

You can observe plant parts. Plan and conduct an investigation to find what you can tell from observing plant parts.

Ask a Question
Record the question.

_____

_____

_____

Materials
Draw and label the materials you will need.

Unit 3 • Plant Parts

Steps Write the steps you will do.

_____

_____

_____

_____

_____

_____

_____

Data

Record your data.

Analyze Your Results
Look for patterns in your data.

Restate Your Question
Write the question you investigated.

_____

_____

_____

Claims, Evidence, and Reasoning
Make a claim that answers your question.

_____

_____

_____

Review the data. What evidence from the investigation supports your claim?

_____

_____

_____

Discuss your reasoning with a partner.

Language Development

As you work through the lessons, fill in the chart using definitions and examples.

Word	What it means
mimic	To copy.
offspring	
parent	

Example	Words I know that are like it
People observed thorns to make fences.	copy

Lesson 1 — Engineer It • What Parts Help Plants Live?

This tree has parts that help it live.

👆 Explore First

Observe a Plant Look at a plant that has been removed from its pot. What parts do you see? Record observations in your Evidence Notebook.

From Seed to Design

Explore Online

Have you ever seen the seed of a maple tree? The seed has wings.

Can You Solve It?

✏️ How did observing the maple seed give people ideas?

_____
_____
_____
_____

Plant Parts

Explore Online

- Seeds form in flowers. Seeds grow into new plants.

- Leaves take in sunlight. Plants need sunlight to live and grow.

- A fruit holds seeds. Fruits grow after flowers make seeds.

- Water moves through the stem to other parts of the plant.

- Roots take up water and hold the plant in the ground.

✏️ Circle a part where seeds are made.

✏️ Put an X on the part that holds the plant.

The parts of a plant help the plant live. The parts work together as a system.

How does the shape of each plant part help the plant live?

Explore Online

Roots have tubes inside. Water moves from soil into the tubes. Stems also have tubes inside.

Leaves have flat, green surfaces that catch sunlight.

Fruits are shaped to hold seeds inside. They protect seeds.

Apply What You Know

Evidence Notebook • Work with a group. Cover the leaf of a plant with dark paper. What do you think will happen to the leaf after two weeks? Use evidence to explain. Record your explanation in your Evidence Notebook.

Light and Leaves

Explore Online

These leaves are very thick. Light can not pass through them. Their shade is very dark.

These leaves are thin. A lot of light passes through them. Their shade is dim.

These leaves block some light, but most light passes through them. Their shade is dim.

Different amounts of light can pass through different leaves.

Do the Math! • Observe leaves. Count how many leaves allow no light through, some light through, and a lot of light through. Show the data in the graph.

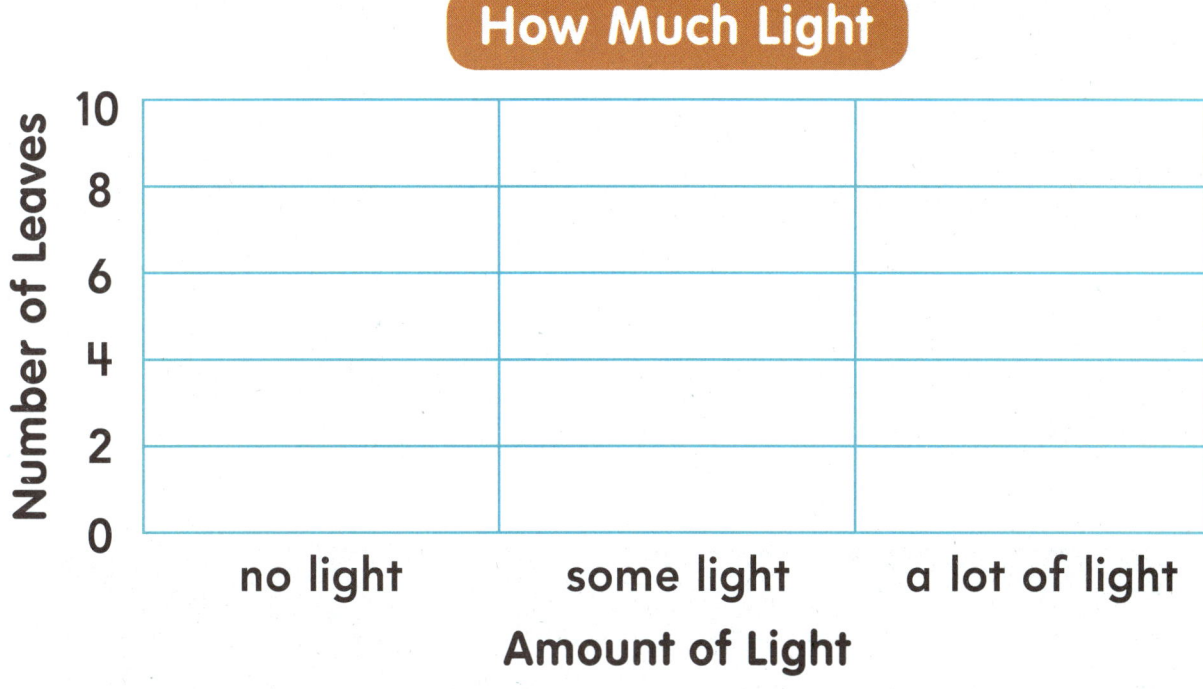

 Apply What You Know

Evidence Notebook • Find a plant outside. Observe when it is covered by shade and when it is not covered by shade. Check the plant at the same time for a few days. Do you see a pattern? Use evidence to describe the pattern.

Looking to Nature

Explore Online

Look at the pictures to see how observing plants can give people ideas.

Leaves take in light to make food for the plant. The solar panels take in sunlight and change it into electricity.

Explore Online

Observing thorns gave people the idea to make barbed wire fences.

People get ideas by observing plants. People **mimic**, or copy, what they see in nature to design things that solve problems.

Lesson 1 • Engineer It • What Parts Help Plants Live?

Which plant did people copy to design the building?

Read, Write, Share! • Work with a partner. Look at pictures of plants. Name solutions that look like those plants. What kind of words does your partner use to describe the solutions? Repeat the words or write them.

Observe Plants

Explore Online

This cactus has folds on its stem. The folds make shade for the plant. The shade keeps the cactus cool in the hot sun.

This tree can tilt its leaves. Then the sun does not hit the leaves directly. That keeps the tree cool.

This cactus shrinks down into the cool desert soil when the weather is hot.

Some plants have ways to keep cool in the heat.

Apply What You Know

Work with a small group. Observe a plant. Talk about its shape and what its parts do. Use ideas from observing the plant to think of a new solution.

✎ Draw and label your solution. Write about how it solves a problem.

_____

_____

_____

_____

Name_____

Hands-On Activity

Engineer It • Observe Plants to Design

Explore Online

Materials • craft materials

Ask a Question

_____

Test and Record Data

Step 1

Explain the problem. Gather information about it.

Step 2

Think about the parts of plants. Plan your solution.

Lesson 1 • Engineer It • What Parts Help Plants Live?

119

Step 3

Build your solution.

Step 4

Share your solution. Explain how observing plant parts gave you an idea for the solution.

Make a claim that answers your question.

What is your evidence?

Take It Further
People in Science & Engineering •
Isabella Abbott

Explore more online.
- Science Writer
- Plants We Eat

Explore Online

coral reef in Hawaii

Isabella Abbott was a botanist from Hawaii. A botanist is a scientist who studies plants. Abbott was interested in ocean plants all her life. She found many new kinds of ocean plants. Abbott also helped protect coral reefs in Hawaii.

Act Like a Botanist

Work with a partner. Find two different kinds of plants in your area. Make observations about the plants. What is different about the plants? What is the same about the plants?

seaweed and fish

 Read, Write, Share!

Record your observations. Summarize your ideas. Use complete sentences.

_____

_____

_____

Lesson Check

Name _____

Can You Solve It?

✏️ How did observing the maple seed give people ideas?

Be sure to
- Tell how observing nature helps people solve problems.

_____
_____
_____
_____
_____

Lesson 1 • Engineer It • What Parts Help Plants Live?

Self Check

1. How are roots and stems alike in a plant part system?

   Ⓐ They make food for the plant.

   Ⓑ They move water to other plant parts.

   Ⓒ They help the plant make new plants.

2. How much light can pass through each leaf? Draw a line to match each leaf to the words that tell how much light.

   | a lot of light | little light | no light |

3. Tari wants to design a way to take the salt out of seawater. Which plant would be best for her to study for ideas?

   Ⓐ a tree that lives in salt water

   Ⓑ a flower that lives in a garden

   Ⓒ a cactus that lives in a desert

4. Which plant did people observe to get the idea for each solution? Draw lines to match the pictures.

5. Look at the seeds on the dog and the hook-and-loop fastener. How are they alike?

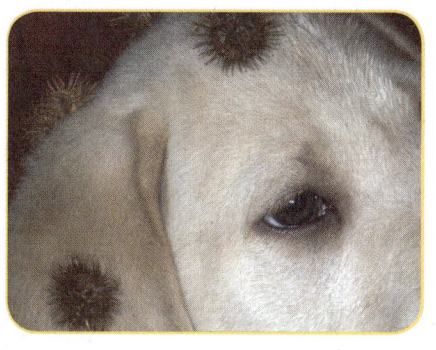

Ⓐ They stick to things.
Ⓑ They take in sunlight.
Ⓒ They are both found in nature.

Lesson 2: How Do Plants Look Like Their Parents?

This field has plants that are of the same kind.

 **Explore First**

Crayon Characteristics Observe crayons. Find things that are the same about the crayons. Discuss what is the same.

Plants of the Same Kind

Explore Online

How are the young plants like the parent plant? How are they different from the parent plant?

young plants

parent plant

Can You Explain It?

✏️ How can you tell if two plants are the same kind of plant?

_____

_____

_____

Young and Old

Explore Online

young trees

parent trees

The young cherry trees do not have flowers yet. They will grow flowers.

A **parent** is a plant or animal that makes young similar to itself. Parent plants make young plants. The young plants may look different from the parent plants. But they will grow to look like the parent plants. **Offspring** are the young of a plant or an animal.

✏️ Circle the parts on the parent tree that are different from the parts on the young tree.

young tree | parent tree

✋ Apply What You Know

Evidence Notebook • Draw pictures to show how a young plant may look different from its parent plant. Use evidence to tell how you know. Then look for patterns in your pictures.

Lesson 2 • How Do Plants Look Like Their Parents?

Compare Parts

Explore Online

How are young plants and parent plants alike and different? Look closely at the pictures.

young plant

parent plant

Most young plants have parts that look like the parts of their parents. The leaves may have the same shape. But the young plants may have smaller or fewer leaves.

🖍 This leaf is from a parent tree. Circle the picture that shows its young.

Apply What You Know

📖 **Read, Write, Share!** • Work in a small group. Choose an adult plant. Research what the plant looks like when it is young. Use headings to find the information you need. Draw a picture to compare the young plant to the adult plant.

Lesson 2 • How Do Plants Look Like Their Parents?

Compare Adult Plants

Explore Online

How are adult plants of the same kind alike and different?

These tulips are different heights.

The flowers of these tulips are different colors.

The leaves on these tulips have the same shape. But the leaves are not the same size.

✏️ This plant is a lily. Circle the picture that also shows a lily.

✋ Apply What You Know

Evidence Notebook • Work in a group. Sort pictures of plants. Which are the same kind of plant? Use patterns you observe to help you. Use evidence to explain how you sorted. Record in your Evidence Notebook.

Lesson 2 • How Do Plants Look Like Their Parents?

Do the Math! • Work with a group. Find three plants. Use connecting cubes to find the height of each plant. Then compare the heights of your plants. Order them from shortest to tallest.

✏️ Draw to show how you ordered. Write about what you did.

_____

_____

_____

Name _____

Hands-On Activity
Grow Carrot Tops

Explore Online

Materials • two carrot tops • small bowl of water

Ask a Question

_____

Test and Record Data

Step 1

Place the bowl of carrots in a sunny place.

Step 2

Observe the carrots each day for ten days. Record your observations.

Lesson 2 • How Do Plants Look Like Their Parents?   135

Step 3

Compare the carrots. Look for patterns in their parts and size.

Step 4

Tell how plants of the same kind are the same and how they are different. Use the patterns you found as evidence.

_____

_____

Make a claim that answers your question.

What is your evidence?

Take It Further
Careers in Science & Engineering •
Soil Scientist

Explore more online.
- Gregor Mendel
- Watch a Pumpkin Grow

Explore Online

Soil scientists use evidence to find out if soil is good for crops. They help farmers decide how to make the soil better for growing plants.

A soil scientist digs holes to see layers underground. The layers show how well the soil soaks up water.

Lesson 2 • How Do Plants Look Like Their Parents?

A soil scientist tests soil.

Read, Write, Share! • Evidence Notebook •

Work with a partner to answer the question, How do soil scientists help farmers? Use evidence to explain your answer. Use words like **before, after,** and **up** to add details to your answer.

✏️ Write your answer.

_____

_____

_____

_____

Lesson Check   Name _____

young plants

Explore Online
parent plant

Can You Explain It?

✏️ How can you tell if two plants are the same kind of plant? Be sure to

- Tell how plants of the same kind can be alike and different.
- Explain how you can observe patterns to tell if two plants are the same kind of plant.

_____
_____
_____
_____

Lesson 2 • How Do Plants Look Like Their Parents?

Self Check

1. How do most young plants and their parent plants look?

    Ⓐ exactly alike

    Ⓑ similar

    Ⓒ very different

2. Observe this young plant and its parent plant. What pattern do you see? Choose all correct answers.

    Ⓐ Their leaves are the same shape.

    Ⓑ Their leaves are purple and green.

    Ⓒ The young plant has more leaves than the parent plant.

    young plant

    parent plant

3. Cate sees a young plant in a park. She wants to find an adult plant that is the same kind of plant. What should Cate look for?

    Ⓐ a plant that is the same size

    Ⓑ a plant with the same number of leaves

    Ⓒ a plant with leaves that are like the young plant's leaves

4. Which plant is the parent of each young plant? Match the young to its parent.

5. Which statements are true? Choose all correct answers.

Ⓐ All tulips are red.

Ⓑ Tulip flowers can be different colors.

Ⓒ Some tulips are taller than others.

Unit Performance Task
Engineer It • Design a House

Materials
- books about water plants
- container of water
- craft materials

STEPS

Step 1

Define a Problem You want to design a house that could be built near or on the water.

Step 2

Plan and Build Look at plants that grow in or near the water. Use ideas from observing the plants to plan at least two solutions. Build your solutions.

Step 3

Test and Improve Test your solutions. How can you improve your solutions?

Step 4

Redesign Make changes to the materials or how you put the materials together. Test your new solutions.

Step 5

Communicate Share your solutions. Compare solutions with others. Use evidence to tell how your solutions solve the problem.

✓ Check

_____ I used ideas from observing plants to plan and build solutions.

_____ I tested my solutions.

_____ I redesigned my solutions.

_____ I shared my solutions with others.

Unit Review

Name _____

1. Look at the plant parts. How do they help the plant? Match the parts to the words.

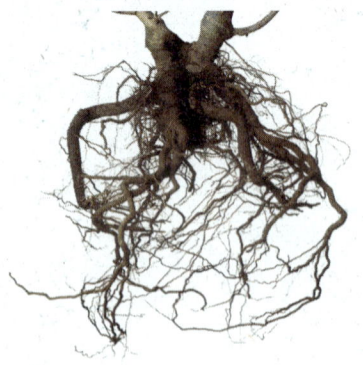  

| make food for the plant | take in water from soil | moves water |

2. How can plants of the same kind be different? Choose all correct answers.

   Ⓐ Their flowers can be different colors.
   Ⓑ They can have different numbers of leaves.
   Ⓒ They can grow different kinds of fruits.

3. Zak found a plant in his yard. He wants to find a young plant of the same kind. What should he look for?

   Ⓐ a smaller plant with bigger leaves.
   Ⓑ a smaller plant with leaves that are the same shape.
   Ⓒ a plant that is the same size.

4. Which plant was the model for each object? Match the object to the plant.

 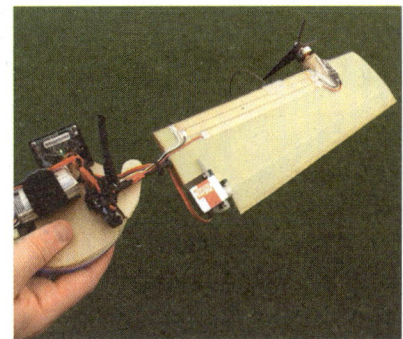 

5. Alonso wants to design a waterproof box that can float. Which plant would be best to study for ideas?
   Ⓐ a plant with seeds that are carried by wind
   Ⓑ a plant with seeds that are carried by water
   Ⓒ a plant with seeds that stick to the fur of animals

6. Which describes how plant parts help a plant? Choose all correct answers.
   Ⓐ Plant parts work together in a system.
   Ⓑ Water moves through a stem to other parts of the plant.
   Ⓒ Flower petals can have different colors.

7. Look at the leaves. Which is true about how much light can pass through the leaves?

   Ⓐ Most light can pass through the leaves.
   Ⓑ Little light can pass through the leaves.
   Ⓒ No light can pass through the leaves.

8. What patterns can you observe to tell if an adult plant and a young plant are of the same kind? Choose all correct answers.
   Ⓐ patterns in leaf shape
   Ⓑ patterns in flower shape
   Ⓒ patterns in stem shape

9. Look at these leaves. Which words describe the leaves? Choose all correct answers.
   Ⓐ No light can pass through the leaves.
   Ⓑ The leaves let a lot of light through.
   Ⓒ The shade of the leaves will be very dark.

10. How does the shape of leaves help leaves catch sunlight?
    Ⓐ Leaves have tubes inside.
    Ⓑ Leaves have wide, flat surfaces.
    Ⓒ Leaves have sharp points.

Unit 4
Animal Parts

Explore Online

You Solve It • Build a Safety Helmet
How can you observe animal parts to get an idea for a helmet? Go online to build a helmet.

Unit 4 At a Glance

Unit Project..........................149

Lesson 1
Engineer It • What Parts Help Animals Live? 154

Lesson 2
How Do Animals Look Like Their Parents? 172

Lesson 3
How Do Animals Take Care of Their Young? 190

Unit Performance Task........206

Unit Review 208

Name _____

Unit Project
Compare Animal Behavior

Think of an animal that can live in the wild and that can also live with people. Compare how the animal cares for its young in the wild and when it is living with people.

Ask a Question
Record the question.

_____

_____

_____

Materials
Draw and label the materials you will need.

Steps Write the steps you will do.

_____

_____

_____

_____

_____

_____

Data

Record your data.

animal living in the wild   animal living with people

Analyze Your Results
Look for patterns in your data.

Restate Your Question
Write the question you investigated.

_____

_____

_____

Claims, Evidence, and Reasoning
Make a claim that answers your question.

_____

_____

_____

Review the data. What evidence from the activity supports your claim?

_____

_____

Discuss your reasoning with a partner.

Language Development

As you work through the lessons, fill in the chart using definitions and examples.

Word	What it means
gills	Body parts that take in oxygen from water.
lungs	
behavior	

Example	Words I know that are like it
the gills of a fish	The part a fish uses to get oxygen.

Lesson 1 Engineer It • What Parts Help Animals Live?

Animals have body parts that help them get food.

 **Explore First**

Animals Around Us Observe animals that live in your area. Draw pictures of the animals. Label parts that help the animals live.

Staying Safe

Explore Online

Have you ever seen a hedgehog?
A hedgehog has spines all over.

Can You Solve It?

✏️ What ideas can you get from observing a hedgehog to keep something safe? Plan a solution.

_____

_____

_____

Animals Use Senses

Explore Online

A prairie dog uses its eyes and nose to notice the things around it. It will warn others if it sees or smells danger.

A great white shark has eyes that see well. It uses its ears to feel movements in the water.

A mouse does not see well at night. It uses its nose to smell for food. It uses its whiskers to feel in the dark.

Moles do not see well. What body parts do you think moles use to notice things and find food? Choose all the correct answers.

Ⓐ nose

Ⓑ eyes

Ⓒ whiskers

 **Apply What You Know**

Evidence Notebook • Work in a group. Talk about how you use your eyes, ears, nose, and hands to notice things around you. Use evidence to tell how you know. Communicate ideas.

Moving Away from Danger

A kangaroo hops on its back legs to stay safe. It uses its tail for balance.

A squirrel climbs to stay safe. It has sharp claws that help it climb.

A dolphin swims fast to stay safe. It uses its tail and flippers to swim.

A butterfly has wings to fly. This makes it hard to catch.

Animals use body parts to move away from danger to stay safe. The shape of the parts allows them to move.

Draw a line to match the animal to the way it moves in order to stay safe.

climbs swims flies

Apply What You Know

 Read, Write, Share! • Evidence Notebook •
Work with a partner. Observe how animals move to stay safe. Write to describe how the animals move. Use words like **runs**, **climbs**, **swims**, or **flies**. Use evidence to tell how you know how they move.

Lesson 1 • Engineer It • What Parts Help Animals Live?

Facing Danger

Explore Online

 A turtle has a hard shell that keeps its body safe.

 A porcupine has sharp quills that keep its body safe.

 An eagle has sharp talons it uses to protect itself.

✏️ Draw a line under the name of the body part that keeps each animal safe.

Some animals have body parts that help them stay safe.

Apply What You Know

Evidence Notebook • Design a box to keep things safe. Use ideas from observing animals. Add parts to your box. Use evidence to explain how its parts and shape keep things safe.

Parts to Eat Food

Explore Online

A bear has sharp claws to grab fish. It has sharp teeth for tearing food.

A frog has a sticky tongue to grab insects. It pulls the insect into its mouth to eat.

Animals use body parts to grab and eat food.

 Apply What You Know

Do the Math! • Work with your class. Learn about human teeth. Find out how many flat teeth and sharp teeth people have. Make a tally chart. Ask and answer questions about the data.

Observe Animals

Explore Online

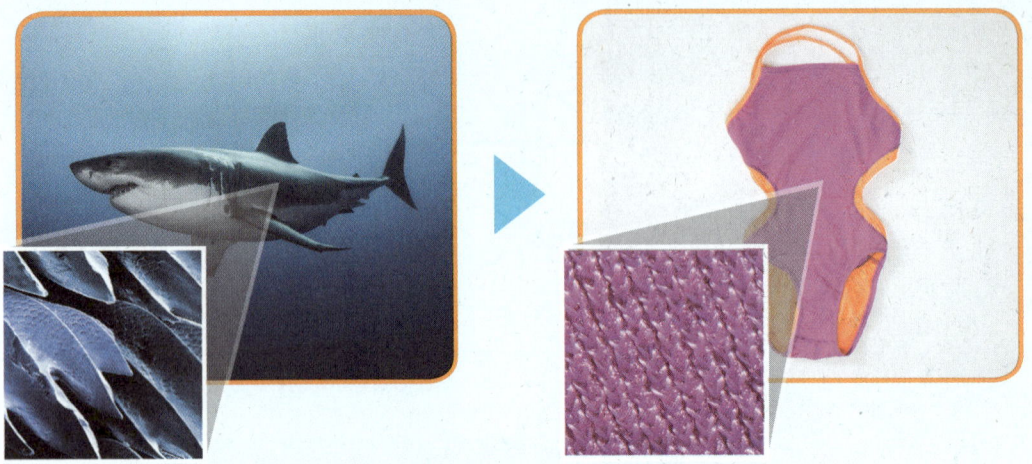

Engineers observed shark scales. They got an idea to make a kind of swimsuit fabric.

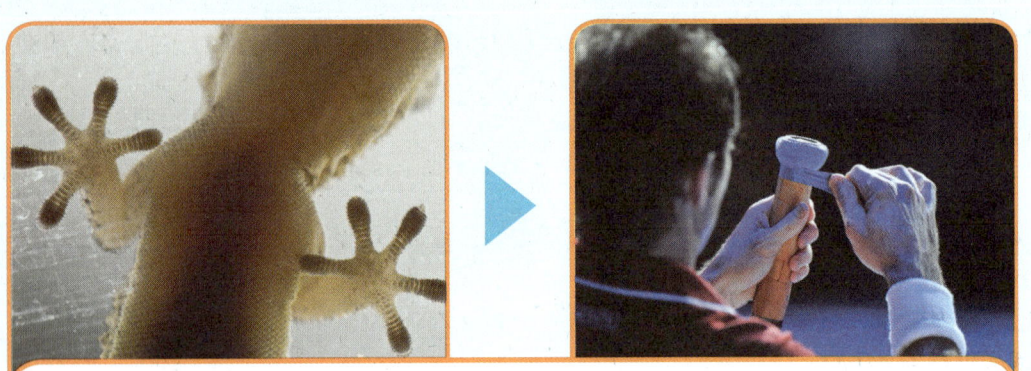

Engineers observed gecko feet. They got an idea to make a tape that does not slip.

Apply What You Know

Do the Math! • Design a paper airplane. Look at pictures of birds for ideas. Measure how far it flies.

Name_____

Hands-On Activity

Engineer It • Observe Animals to Design

Explore Online

Materials • animal books • craft materials

Ask a Question

_____

Test and Record Data

Step 1

Look in animal books. Observe how animals use their body parts to pick up food.

Step 2

Plan and build two solutions for picking up food.

Lesson 1 • Engineer It • What Parts Help Animals Live?

Step 3

Test your tool. Compare it with the tools of other classmates. How did observing animals give you an idea to solve the problem?

Make a claim that answers your question.

_____

_____

_____

_____

What is your evidence?

_____

_____

_____

Parts to Breathe and Take in Water

Explore Online

A fish has gills. **Gills** are body parts that take in oxygen from water. Many animals that live in water have gills.

A zebra has lungs. **Lungs** are body parts that take in oxygen from air. Most land animals have lungs.

Animals need to take in oxygen. They have different body parts to help them take in oxygen.

Explore Online

An elephant uses its trunk to take in water. Then it moves the water into its mouth.

A fish lives in water. Its body needs water, too. A fish takes in water through its skin and gills.

Animals need water to live. They have different body parts to take in water.

Apply What You Know

 Read, Write, Share! • Look in books with a partner. Find one animal that uses lungs and one animal that uses gills. Use evidence to tell how you know. Communicate your ideas to your partner.

Take It Further
Careers in Science & Engineering •
Bioengineer

Explore more online.
- Miguel Mora
- New Body Parts for Animals

Explore Online

A bioengineer is a kind of engineer. Bioengineers design things to help people. They also look for ways to help the environment.

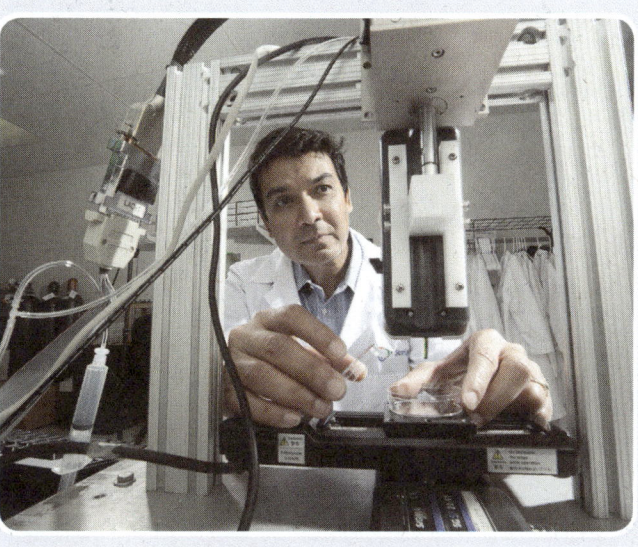

Bioengineers can work in labs. They make new medicines to help people who are ill.

Bioengineers find new ways to clean air and water. They also help farmers grow food in ways that are safer.

What does a bioengineer do? Choose all correct answers.

Ⓐ helps clean air and water
Ⓑ studies rocks
Ⓒ makes new medicine

Lesson Check

Name _____

Can You Solve It?

✏️ What ideas can you get from observing a hedgehog to keep something safe? Plan a solution. Be sure to

- Tell how a hedgehog's body parts keep it safe.
- Describe how observing the hedgehog gave you an idea for a solution.

_____

_____

_____

_____

Self Check

1. How does the shape of the claws of a squirrel help the squirrel?

    Ⓐ The claws are sharp for climbing.
    Ⓑ The claws are flat for balancing.
    Ⓒ The claws are smooth for swimming.

2. What body part keeps a turtle safe from other animals?

    Ⓐ legs
    Ⓑ shell
    Ⓒ fur

3. Which animals would you use as models to design a solution that helps you swim faster? Circle the animals.

4. Which animal was used as a model for each object? Match the object to the animal.

5. Which material would you use to act like blubber? Choose the best answer.

Ⓐ rubber

Ⓑ wood

Ⓒ plastic

Lesson 2: How Do Animals Look Like Their Parents?

A young koala looks like its parent.

 **Explore First**

Animal Families Observe pictures of animal adults and their young. Explain how the adults are the same as their young. Explain how they are different from their young. Use evidence.

Related Animals

Explore Online

Look at the adult swan and her young. What can you tell about the birds?

Can You Explain It?

✏️ You see a young animal. You want to find an adult animal that is of the same kind. What should you look for?

_____

_____

_____

Lesson 2 • How Do Animals Look Like Their Parents?

Animals Grow

Explore Online

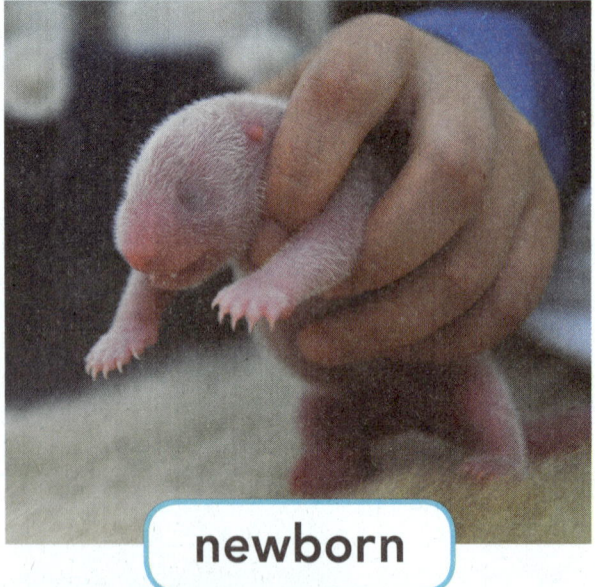
newborn

3 weeks old

3 months old

1 year old

Parent animals make young animals similar to themselves. Young animals are smaller than their parents. They will grow to look like their parents. Look at how a panda changes as it grows into an adult.

adult

What is the same about a panda that is three months old and a panda that is an adult? Choose all correct answers.

Ⓐ They are the same size.
Ⓑ They have the same color fur.
Ⓒ They are the same shape.

 Apply What You Know

Evidence Notebook • Draw pictures to show an animal when it is young and when it is an adult. Talk with a partner about your animal. How does it grow and change? Use evidence to tell how you know. Look for patterns in your pictures.

Lesson 2 • How Do Animals Look Like Their Parents?

Compare Parts

Explore Online

An elephant parent has big ears and a long trunk. A young elephant has big ears and a long trunk, too.

This young rhino looks a lot like its parent, but it does not have a horn. It will grow a horn like its parent.

Think about young animals. How can you tell what kind of animal they are? One way is to look at their body parts. Most young animals have parts like their parents.

Name _____

Hands-On Activity
Observe Brine Shrimp

Explore Online

Materials
- container with water
- brine shrimp eggs
- hand lens

Ask a Question

_____

Test and Record Data

Step 1

Add the brine shrimp eggs to the water.

Step 2

Observe the brine shrimp every other day for two weeks. Record your observations.

Lesson 2 • How Do Animals Look Like Their Parents?

Step 3

Compare the size, shape, and parts of the brine shrimp. How are the brine shrimp the same? How are they different? Use the patterns you found as evidence.

_____

_____

Make a claim that answers your question.

_____

_____

_____

What is your evidence?

_____

_____

_____

✏️ This is a young anteater. Circle the picture below that shows an adult anteater.

Apply What You Know

Evidence Notebook • Observe animals. What body parts does each animal have? How can you tell if the animal is young or an adult? Use evidence to tell how you know. Record your answers in your Evidence Notebook.

Lesson 2 • How Do Animals Look Like Their Parents?

Compare Body Coverings

Explore Online

Some body coverings are scales, fur, or feathers. How are the body coverings of young animals and their parents alike and different?

young raccoon

adult raccoon

Raccoons have dark fur around their eyes. The young and the adult have the same color fur.

young chicken

adult chicken

A young chick has yellow, fluffy feathers. It will grow new feathers and look more like its parent.

✏️ Observe each animal. Then draw a line to match each parent animal to its young.

Apply What You Know

📖 **Read, Write, Share!** • Choose an animal. Observe what its covering looks like when it is young and when it is an adult. Talk with classmates about how the coverings are alike and different. Use complete sentences.

Lesson 2 • How Do Animals Look Like Their Parents?

Animals of the Same Kind

Explore Online

How can animals of the same kind be alike and different?

These fish are all the same kind. They have the same body parts, but they are not the same size. They also have different colors and markings.

These dogs are all the same kind. They all have four legs and a tail. They all have fur, but their fur is different colors.

✏️ Look at the animals. Circle the two that are the same kind of animal. Look for patterns.

Do the Math! • Compare the dogs. Put them in order from shortest to tallest. Write 1, 2, or 3.

_____   _____   _____

 Apply What You Know

Evidence Notebook • Work with a partner. Look through books for animals of the same kind. Tell how they are alike and different. Use evidence to tell how you know. Draw the animals in your Evidence Notebook.

Take It Further
People in Science & Engineering •
Robyn Hannigan

Explore more online.
- The Butterfly Life Cycle
- Pet Investigation

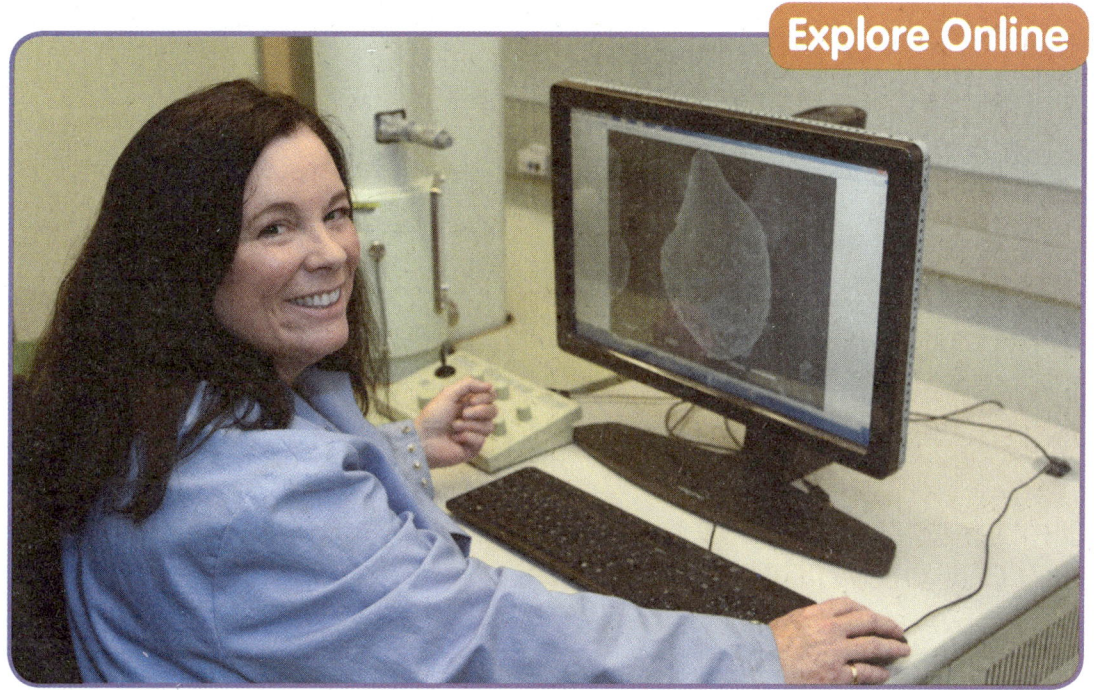

Robyn Hannigan is an environmental scientist. She has studied patterns in the ear bones of fish. The patterns tell how fast fish grow. Studying ear bones can also show where fish have lived. Hannigan has used her research to help make fishing rules.

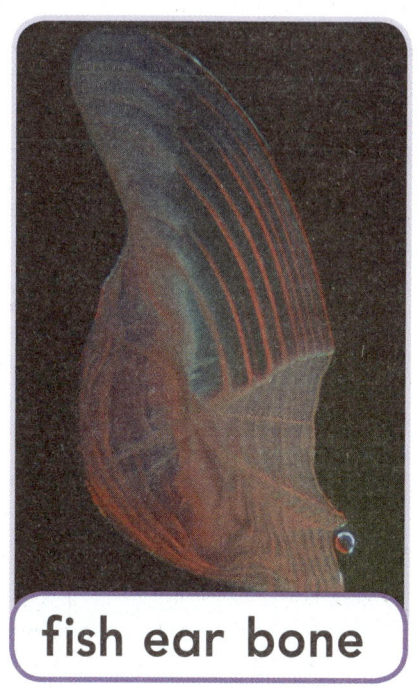

fish ear bone

Read, Write, Share!

What kinds of things might affect how quickly or slowly a fish grows? Write your ideas.

Do research. Does the information you find support your ideas?

Chinook salmon

Draw or write about your ideas.

_____

_____

_____

Lesson Check

Name _____

Explore Online

Can You Explain It?

✏️ You see a young animal. You want to find an adult animal that is of the same kind. What should you look for? Be sure to

- Tell how animals of the same kind can be alike and different.
- Explain how you can observe patterns to tell if two animals are the same kind of animal.

_____
_____
_____
_____

Self Check

1. Which is **true** about most young animals and their parents? Choose all correct answers.

    Ⓐ Young animals have parts like their parents.

    Ⓑ Young animals grow to look like their parents.

    Ⓒ Young animals are bigger than their parents.

2. Marco observes a young animal that has scales on its body. What will the young animal's parent likely have?

    Ⓐ fur

    Ⓑ scales

    Ⓒ a shell

3. Observe each young animal and its parent. What pattern do you see?

    Ⓐ They are the same size.

    Ⓑ They have the same pattern on their fur.

    Ⓒ They have different body parts.

4. Which animal is the parent of each young? Match the parent to its young.

5. Amy observes two dogs that are of the same kind. Which sentences could be true about the dogs?

Ⓐ The dogs are different colors.

Ⓑ One dog has fur and one dog has feathers.

Ⓒ One dog is smaller than the other dog.

Lesson 3: How Do Animals Take Care of Their Young?

Animals care for their young in different ways.

Explore First

Helping Young What do adults do for small children? Record your ideas. How is this similar or different from the way animals care for their young? Compare.

Animals Help Their Young

Have you ever seen a frog with a tadpole on its back? This frog carries its tadpole up a tree. It puts the tadpole in water inside a flower.

Can You Explain It?

How do animals help their young survive?

_____

_____

_____

Staying Safe

Explore Online

A **behavior** is a way an animal acts. What are some behaviors that help keep young animals safe?

Young rabbits hide in grass while their mother is away. They wait for their mother to come back. They listen for her to call and then call back to her.

A father penguin holds his young on his feet. This keeps his young warm.

✏️ **Draw a line to match the animals to the words that tell how the young stay safe.**

hide to stay safe   held on feet of parent

Lesson 3 • How Do Animals Take Care of Their Young?

Do the Math! • One wolf spider carries 64 eggs in an egg sac. Another wolf spider carries 48 eggs. Which number of spider eggs is larger?
Write <, >, or =.

64 ◯ 48

Apply What You Know

Evidence Notebook • Work with classmates. Find pictures of animals and their young staying safe. Talk about what the animals do to stay safe. Use evidence. Make a chart to show patterns.

Finding Food

Young gulls peck the bill of a parent when they are hungry.

Meerkats live in groups. Young meerkats call to adults to bring them food. They stay close to the adults who bring them the most food.

Young animals show behaviors that help them get food from their parents. Young animals may show a behavior in a group system to get food from adults.

🖍 Which young animal shows a behavior in a group system to get food? Circle the correct picture.

✋ Apply What You Know

Evidence Notebook • Observe animals around your school. How are the animals working in a system to find food and survive? Use evidence to tell how you know. Talk with a partner. Record what you observe.

Young Animals Learn

Bear cubs learn to catch fish for food.

Leopard cubs learn to move around to stay safe.

Some young animals learn from their parents. They stay with their parents for a few years. They watch what their parents do to find food and stay safe.

What is this orangutan teaching its young to do?

Ⓐ find fruit

Ⓑ hide in a shelter

Ⓒ catch small animals

✋ Apply What You Know

 Read, Write, Share! • Think about how different animal parents take care of their young. Work with a partner to answer these questions, How do the animals act the same? How do they act differently?

Name_____

Hands-On Activity
Compare How Animals Learn

Explore Online

Materials • a computer   • animal books

Ask a Question

_____

Test and Record Data

Step 1

Work with a partner. Research polar bears and lions. Use a computer and animal books to collect information.

Step 2

Find out how polar bears and lions teach their young to find food. Find out how they teach their young to stay safe.

Lesson 3 • How Do Animals Take Care of Their Young?

Step 3

Write or draw pictures to show what you found. Look for patterns in how the young animals learn from their parents.

_____
_____
_____
_____

Make a claim that answers your question.

_____
_____
_____

What is your evidence?

_____
_____

Take It Further

People in Science & Engineering
David Mizejewski

Explore more online.
- Wildlife Conservationist
- Pet Investigation

Explore Online

David Mizejewski loved playing outside as a boy. Now, he is a wildlife expert. He teaches people about protecting the environment. He wrote a book about how to plant gardens that provide food and shelter for wildlife. These kinds of gardens help wildlife survive.

Plan a Garden

Work with a partner. Plan a garden where wildlife in your area can live. Look for the plants that you will use in the garden.

▬▶ Draw a plan for your garden and label it.

_____

_____

_____

Lesson Check

Name _____

Can You Explain It?

✏️ How do animals help their young survive? Be sure to

- Describe patterns in how some animals act to take care of their young.
- Explain how this helps the young survive.

_____

_____

_____

_____

Self Check

1. Which are behaviors that help young animals? Choose all correct answers.

    Ⓐ A gull feeds its young.

    Ⓑ A rabbit calls to its young.

    Ⓒ A penguin keeps its young warm.

2. How do these young animals act so they can get food? Choose all correct answers.

    Ⓐ The young call to the adults.

    Ⓑ The young show a behavior in a group system.

    Ⓒ The young peck at the adults.

3. Observe each bird and its young. What pattern do you see?

Ⓐ The parent bird is teaching its young to fly.

Ⓑ The parent bird is feeding its young.

Ⓒ The parent bird and its young are staying safe.

4. Which is an example of young animals showing a behavior in a group system?

Ⓐ A young gull pecks at a parent.

Ⓑ A bear cub learns to catch fish from a parent.

Ⓒ A young meerkat stays close to adults that bring it the most food.

5. How long do bear cubs and leopard cubs stay with their mothers?

Ⓐ a few days

Ⓑ a few weeks

Ⓒ a few years

Lesson 3 • How Do Animals Take Care of Their Young?

Unit Performance Task

Match Animals and Their Young

Materials
- animal cards
- pencil
- scissors

STEPS

Step 1

Cut ten animal cards from the paper.

Step 2

Put the cards face down on a table.

Step 3

Ask a classmate to turn over two cards. It is a match if the cards show an adult animal and its young.

Step 4

Tell how the adult and young are alike and different.

Step 5

Take turns flipping over the cards until all the adults and young are matched.

Step 6

What patterns do you observe? Write the patterns.

✓ Check

_____ I cut ten animal cards.
_____ I played a matching game.
_____ I compared animals and their young.
_____ I wrote the patterns I observed.

Unit Review

Name _____

1. Which solution mimics a bird's beak that grabs food?

Ⓐ   Ⓑ   Ⓒ

2. Tamara wants to design a solution that will protect her head. Which shape should she mimic for her solution?
   Ⓐ the shape of a porcupine quill
   Ⓑ the shape of a turtle shell
   Ⓒ the shape of an eagle talon

3. Which body parts do animals use to take in oxygen? Choose all correct answers.
   Ⓐ lungs
   Ⓑ gills
   Ⓒ fins

4. Which animal is the parent of each young? Look for patterns. Match the young to its parent.

5. Kim sees an animal with fur on its body. What will a young animal of the same kind have on its body?
   Ⓐ feathers
   Ⓑ a shell
   Ⓒ fur

6. Which is true about young animals and their parents? Choose all correct answers.
   Ⓐ Young animals are smaller than their parents.
   Ⓑ Young animals are always different colors from their parents.
   Ⓒ Young animals are the same kind of animal as their parents.

Unit 4 • Animal Parts

7. Bella sees two horses that are the same kind, but they do not look exactly alike. How might they be different?

Ⓐ They have different body coverings.

Ⓑ They are different sizes.

Ⓒ They have different numbers of legs.

8. Which is an example of how adult animals care for young in a group system? Choose all correct answers.

Ⓐ A mother gull feeds a young gull.

Ⓑ A group of adult elephants protect a young elephant.

Ⓒ Meerkat adults bring food to young meerkats.

9. Which animals are feeding their young? Look for patterns. Choose all correct answers.

Unit 5
Animal Sounds

Explore Online

You Solve It • Getting the Band Together
How can you vibrate parts of instruments to make sound? Go online to make instruments.

Unit 5 At a Glance

Unit Project..................................... 213

Lesson 1
What Is Sound? 218

Lesson 2
Engineer It • How Do Animals Make Sounds? 234

Unit Performance Task 250

Unit Review 252

Name _____

 **Unit Project**
Explore Sound

Think about how sound is made. Plan and conduct an investigation to find out if there is a connection between things that vibrate and sound.

Ask a Question
Record the question.

_____

_____

_____

Materials
Draw and label the materials you will need.

Steps Write the steps you will do.

_____
_____
_____
_____
_____
_____
_____
_____

Data

Record your data.

throat _____

kazoo _____

speaker _____

Analyze Your Results
Look for patterns in your data.

Restate Your Question
Write the question you investigated.

_____

_____

_____

Claims, Evidence, and Reasoning
Make a claim that answers your question.

_____

_____

Review the data. What evidence from the investigation supports your claim?

_____

_____

_____

Discuss your reasoning with a partner.

 # Language Development

As you work through the lessons, fill in the chart using definitions and examples.

Word	What it means
sound	A kind of energy you hear when something vibrates.
vibrate	
volume	
pitch	
communicate	

Example	Words I know that are like it
singing	noise

Lesson 1: What Is Sound?

Sound can make materials move.

Explore First

Sound Game Listen to sounds. Describe how the sounds are different. Classify the sounds. Use evidence to explain how you classified.

Make Objects Move

Explore Online

A speaker makes sound. Look at what happens when water is placed over the speaker.

Can You Explain It?

✏️ Why does the water move?

_____

_____

_____

Make a Sound

Sounds are all around you, but what is sound? **Sound** is a kind of energy that you hear when something vibrates. To **vibrate** is to move quickly back and forth.

A hammer in the piano hits a string.

The string vibrates, or moves. It makes a sound you can hear.

When does a piano string make sound?

Ⓐ when it travels

Ⓑ when it vibrates

Ⓒ when it listens

👋 Apply What You Know

Work with a group. Hold a metal ruler down on a table. Let half of the ruler hang over the edge of the table. Pluck the part of the ruler sticking out. What do you hear? Do tests to make different sounds. What causes the sound to change?

Lesson 1 • What Is Sound?

Volume and Pitch

Explore Online

A siren makes a loud sound.

A whisper is a soft sound.

What is the difference between a siren and a whisper? They have different volumes. One is loud and one is soft. **Volume** is how loud or soft a sound is.

low pitch

high pitch

Sounds can also be high or low. **Pitch** is how high or low a sound is. You can hear a high pitch and a low pitch on a piano. The keys on one side of a piano make low sounds. The keys on the other side of a piano make high sounds.

✏️ Look at the pictures. Write **loud** or **soft** to tell about the sound each thing makes.

_____   _____

_____   _____

✏️ Write **high** or **low** to complete the sentence. The sound of thunder has a _____ pitch.

Do the Math! • Pitch is measured with hertz. Hertz is a measurement for sound. A tuba can play a note with a pitch of 32 hertz. A cello can play a note with a pitch of 65 hertz.

Compare the numbers. Write <, >, or =.

32  65

Apply What You Know

 Read, Write, Share! • Explore pitch in your classroom. Find objects that make sounds with a high pitch. Find objects that make sounds with a low pitch. Write about how you found the objects. Make a table to organize your information. Share your table with other classmates.

What Makes It Move?

Explore Online

Look at the pictures. When the speaker is off, there is no sound. The balloon does not move. What happens when the speaker is on and sound begins to play? Sound waves from the speaker hit the balloon. The balloon moves.

Apply What You Know

Evidence Notebook • Work with a partner. Use a tuning fork and a glass of water to explore sound. Plan a test to show that sound can make materials vibrate. Use evidence to tell what happened.

Name _____

Hands-On Activity

Make Something Move with Sound

Explore Online

Materials
- a metal can
- cling wrap
- a rubber band
- rice
- a pot
- a wooden spoon

Ask a Question

_____

Test and Record Data

Step 1

Make a drum. Now put a handful of rice on top of the drum.

Step 2

Do the test. Bang a pot loudly very close to the drum.

Step 3

Record what you observe. Did the sound from the pot move the rice?

Lesson 1 • What Is Sound?

Step 4

Explain why the rice did or did not move.
Identify cause and effect.

Make a claim that answers your question.

_____

_____

_____

What is your evidence?

_____

_____

_____

Take It Further
People in Science & Engineering
José Hernández-Rebollar

Explore more online.
- Sound Designer
- Pitch In!

Explore Online

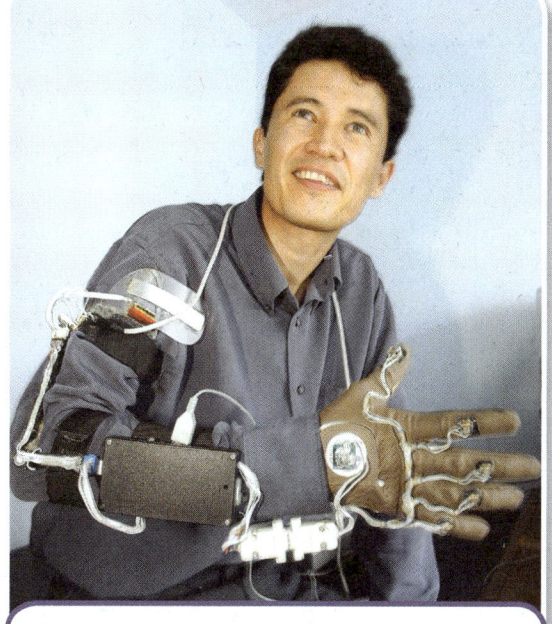

Hernández-Rebollar

José Hernández-Rebollar is an engineer. He designed a glove. The glove turns American Sign Language into spoken and written words. The glove can sense how people move their hands.

communicating in American Sign Language

Design a Doorbell

Work with a partner. Design a doorbell for people who can not hear. Draw and label the doorbell. Explain how the doorbell works.

✏️ Draw and write to explain.

_____
_____
_____
_____

Lesson Check

Name _____

Explore Online

Can You Explain It?

✏️ Why does the water move?

Be sure to

- Describe how sound can affect materials.
- Explain what causes the water to move.

_____

_____

_____

_____

Lesson 1 • What Is Sound?

Self Check

1. What causes sound?
   - Ⓐ pitch
   - Ⓑ energy when something vibrates
   - Ⓒ volume

2. What is the main way the sounds of a siren and a whisper are different?
   - Ⓐ They have different pitches.
   - Ⓑ They are different kinds of energy.
   - Ⓒ They have different volumes.

3. Which pictures show that sound is made when something vibrates? Circle all correct answers.

 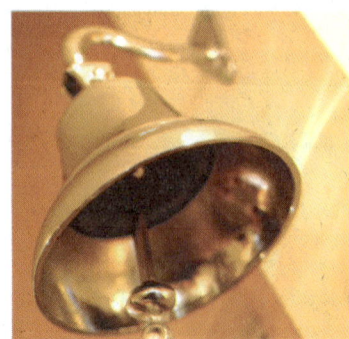 

4. Can sound make materials move? Which test should you do to answer the question?

 Ⓐ pluck a guitar string

 Ⓑ bang a pot near a pile of rice

 Ⓒ blow across the top of a water bottle

5. Tim plans and does the test shown in the picture. What does this tuning fork test tell Tim?

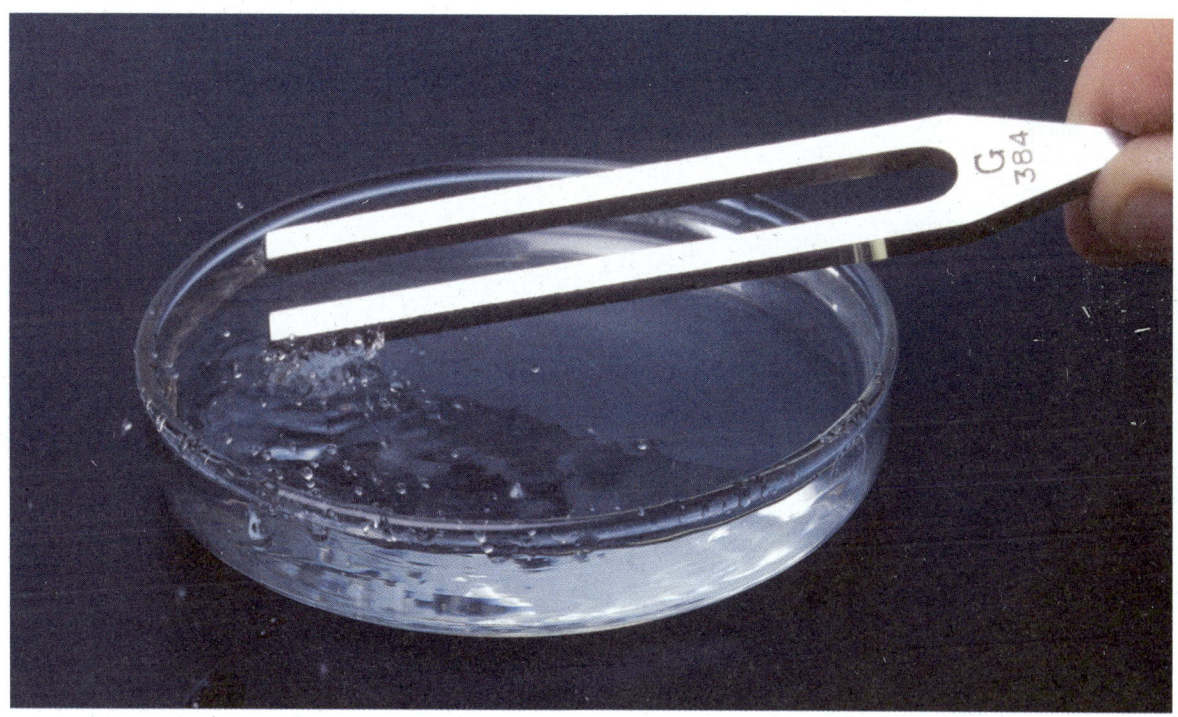

 Ⓐ Sound can make materials move.

 Ⓑ Sounds can have high or low pitch.

 Ⓒ Sounds can be loud or soft.

Lesson 2 • Engineer It • How Do Animals Make Sounds?

Birds make sounds to communicate.

Explore First

Make It Vibrate Place two fingers on your throat. Then hum or speak. Do you feel your throat vibrate? How is this connected to the sound you make? Record your observations in your Evidence Notebook.

Communicating Danger

Explore Online

Have you ever seen an animal stand like this? This animal is communicating to its group.

Can You Explain It?

✏️ How do the other animals know there is danger?

_____

_____

_____

Parts That Vibrate

Explore Online

A cricket scrapes its two front wings together. The wings vibrate. This makes a sound.

A rattlesnake shakes its tail. This makes the parts at the tip of its tail vibrate. This makes a sound.

Animals can make sound. Parts of their body vibrate to make sound.

✏️ This insect is a katydid. It makes sound in the same way as a cricket. Circle the parts of a katydid that vibrate to make sound.

✋ Apply What You Know

Look at pictures of crickets. Then draw a model of a cricket. Label its body parts. Identify the parts that vibrate to make sound. How does the shape of the parts allow the cricket to make sound?

Sounds Make a Message

Explore Online

Coyotes make calls to communicate. Some calls tell their family to come together.

Prairie dogs make calls to communicate that there is danger. Patterns in the calls tell other prairie dogs what kind of danger is near.

Animals make sounds to communicate with each other. **Communicate** means to share information. Animals work together in a system to communicate.

California tree frog

A California tree frog makes a call to find other animals. The call has a sound with a low pitch.

California quail

A California quail makes a call to find other animals. The call has a sound with a high pitch.

Some animals make sounds to find other animals of the same kind. Then these animals can become parents and have young.

✏️ Why do coyotes make calls? Draw a line from the picture to the correct answer.

to communicate with their family

to find shelter

✋ Apply What You Know

Evidence Notebook • Work with a partner. Choose an animal. What body parts does it use to make sound? How does sound help the animal communicate? Use evidence to tell others about your animal and its sounds.

Keep in Touch

Explore Online

Elephants make different sounds to communicate. They make a low sound to tell other elephants to move in a certain direction.

These birds make calls as they fly over distances. The calls help keep groups of birds together.

Some animals make sounds to keep their group together. The group of animals is a system.

Lesson 2 • Engineer It • How Do Animals Make Sounds?

Do the Math! • Work with a group to make string phones. Test the phones. Try different lengths of string. Measure the strings with your feet. Did the length of the string affect the sound? Use evidence to tell how you know.

 Record your answer.

_____

_____

_____

 Apply What You Know

Read, Write, Share! • **Evidence Notebook** • Talk to a partner about animal sounds. Why do animals make sounds? What body parts do they use? Use words like **so** and **because** to connect your ideas. Use evidence to explain.

Name_____

Hands-On Activity
Engineer It • Communicate over Distance

Explore Online

> **Materials**
> • an object that makes noise   • craft materials

Ask a Question

_____

_____

Test and Record Data

Step 1

Go outside with your object. Have your partner walk 50 steps away from you.

Step 2

Make sound with your object. Use different volumes and patterns to communicate different things to your partner.

Lesson 2 • Engineer It • How Do Animals Make Sounds?

Step 3

Plan and build something that makes your sound louder. Repeat steps 1 and 2 to test your solution.

Step 4

Record what you observed. Tell how you used your model to show how animals communicate.

_____

_____

Make a claim that answers your question.

_____

_____

_____

What is your evidence?

_____

_____

_____

Take It Further
Careers in Science & Engineering •
Ethologist

Explore more online.
- Maydianne Andrade
- Hear Like a Bat

Explore Online

Jane Goodall observing chimpanzees

How do animals communicate and learn? Ethologists observe them to find out how. They observe how animals communicate in the wild. They may also study animals that live with people.

Lesson 2 • Engineer It • How Do Animals Make Sounds?

Read, Write, Share!

How do ethologists help us understand what animals do? Write to answer the question. Use words like **in** and **when** to add details to your answer.

ethologist observing a parrot

✏️ Write your answer.

_____

_____

_____

_____

Lesson Check

Name _____

Can You Explain It?

✏️ How do the other animals know there is danger? Be sure to

- Describe how animals use sound to communicate.
- Explain how animals work together in a system to communicate.

_____

_____

_____

Lesson 2 • Engineer It • How Do Animals Make Sounds?

Self Check

1. Keith draws a model to show how a rattlesnake makes sound. He wants to label the part of the snake that vibrates.
   Which part should he label?

   Ⓐ the tail
   Ⓑ the eyes
   Ⓒ the head

2. Jess wants to design an instrument with parts that scrape to make sound. Which animal model should Jess observe for ideas?

   Ⓐ an elephant
   Ⓑ a cricket
   Ⓒ a coyote

3. Which is an example of how animals work together in a system to communicate? Choose all correct answers.

   Ⓐ Elephants make a sound to keep their group together.
   Ⓑ Prairie dogs make a sound to warn each other.
   Ⓒ Coyotes make a sound to gather their family.

4. Alejandro wants to make a tool that shows how these birds communicate with sound. What should his tool be able to do?

Ⓐ communicate very quietly
Ⓑ communicate over a distance
Ⓒ communicate in the dark

5. Why do animals make sounds to communicate? Choose all correct answers.

Ⓐ to warn about danger
Ⓑ to keep groups together
Ⓒ to find other animals

Unit Performance Task
Communicate with Sound

Materials
- musical instruments

STEPS

Step 1
Does your school have a bell that rings at the start of the day? Make a list of the sounds your school uses to communicate messages. Talk about the list with others.

Step 2
Think of ways you can use sounds to communicate with another class. Plan what materials you will use.

Step 3
Decide what different sounds and patterns of sound will mean. Make a list to help people learn the sounds and their meanings.

Step 4

Test your sound signals. Can others understand your message?

Step 5

Compare your plan with the plans of your classmates. Talk about how they are alike and different.

✔ **Check**

_____ I talked about the sounds my school uses to communicate.

_____ I planned which materials I would use to communicate with sound.

_____ I made a list of what my different sounds mean.

_____ I tested my sound signals with others.

_____ I compared my plan to other plans.

Unit Review

Name _____

1. What happens when something vibrates? Choose all correct answers.
    Ⓐ It moves back and forth quickly.
    Ⓑ It can make sound.
    Ⓒ It can make materials move.

2. Beth thinks that materials that vibrate can make sound. Which test should she do to see this?
    Ⓐ She should listen to sounds in her neighborhood.
    Ⓑ She should boil a pot of water.
    Ⓒ She should pluck a guitar string.

3. Write **loud** or **soft** to tell the volume of the sound in each picture.

_____   _____

_____   _____

4. Which sound has a high pitch?
   Ⓐ a growling dog
   Ⓑ a squeaky wheel
   Ⓒ a purring cat

5. Which pictures show how sound can move materials?

   Ⓐ  Ⓑ  Ⓒ

6. Gerard wants to do a test to show that sound can move materials. Which test should he do?
   Ⓐ place sand on a drum and bang a pot next to it
   Ⓑ pour a cup of sand into a large pot
   Ⓒ put sand in a shaker and shake it

7. Claudia wants to design a tool that mimics how a rattlesnake makes sound. What should her tool do?
   Ⓐ Her tool should have parts that scrape together.
   Ⓑ Her tool should make other materials move.
   Ⓒ Her tool should have parts that shake.

8. Which is an example of animals using sound in a group system to stay safe?
   Ⓐ A young bird chirps because it is hungry.
   Ⓑ A prairie dog makes a call to warn other prairie dogs about danger.
   Ⓒ Tree frogs make calls to find other animals of the same kind.

9. Angelina makes a model to show how a cricket makes noise. She wants to label the part of the cricket that vibrates. Which part of the cricket should she label? Circle the part.

10. How does making sound help animals become parents?
    Ⓐ Animals make sound to find each other.
    Ⓑ Animals make sound because they are hungry.
    Ⓒ Animals make sound because they are in danger.

Unit 6
Objects and Patterns in the Sky

Explore Online

You Solve It • Eyes on the Sky
Can you observe a pattern of the phases of the moon? Go online to explore more.

Unit 6 At a Glance

Unit Project 257

Lesson 1
What Are Patterns of Objects in the Sky? 262

Lesson 2
What Are Patterns of Daylight? 280

Unit Performance Task 296

Unit Review 298

Name _____

 **Unit Project**
Explore the Moon's Phases

You can make a model of the phases of the moon. Plan and conduct an investigation to find out what causes the phases of the moon.

Ask a Question
Record the question.

_____

_____

_____

Materials
Draw and label the materials you will need.

Unit 6 • Objects and Patterns in the Sky

Steps Write the steps you will do.

_____

_____

_____

_____

_____

_____

_____

_____

Data

Record your data.

Analyze Your Results

How does using the model help explain the moon's phases?

Restate Your Question

Write the question you investigated.

_____

_____

_____

Claims, Evidence, and Reasoning

Make a claim that answers your question.

_____

_____

_____

Review the data. What evidence from the investigation supports your claim?

_____

_____

_____

Discuss your reasoning with a partner.

🦋 Language Development

As you work through the lessons, fill in the chart using definitions and examples.

Word	What it means
star	An object in the sky that gives off its own light.
sun	
moon	
phases	
season	

Example	Words I know that are like it
The small spots of light I see in the sky at night.	sun

Lesson 1: What Are Patterns of Objects in the Sky?

Objects in the nighttime sky seem to change.

Explore First

Sky Sorting Go outside. List objects you see in the daytime sky. Record your observations in your Evidence Notebook. Compare these objects to objects you might see in the nighttime sky.

Objects in the Sky

Explore Online

Look at the pictures of the sky at different times.

daytime

nighttime

Can You Explain It?

How do objects in the sky seem to change?

_____

_____

_____

_____

The Daytime Sky

Explore Online

sun from Earth

sun close up

You can see objects in the daytime sky. You may see the sun and sometimes the moon. The sun is a star. A **star** is an object in the sky. It gives off its own light. The **sun** is the star closest to Earth. It is made of hot gases. It gives off light and heat.

 Underline two sentences that tell facts about the sun.

Apply What You Know

Evidence Notebook • Work with a partner. Talk about what you know about the sun in the daytime sky. Use evidence to tell how you know. Then write sentences about it in your Evidence Notebook.

Patterns in the Daytime Sky **Explore Online**

In early morning, the sun seems low in the sky.

At noon, the sun seems to be directly above us.

By late afternoon, it seems to be low again, but on the other side of the sky. This pattern repeats each day.

Each day, Earth turns all the way around. This makes the sun seem to move across the sky.

✏️ Match each picture to the word or words that describe it.

early morning

noon

late afternoon

Name_____

Hands-On Activity
Observe the Pattern of the Sun

Explore Online

Materials • drawing paper

Ask a Question

_____

Test and Record Data

Step 1

Choose a time in the morning. Record the time.

_____

Step 2

Go outside. Draw a picture to record the position of the sun. Be sure not to look directly at the sun.

Step 3

Look for an object that makes a shadow. Draw a picture of the object and its shadow.

Lesson 1 • What Are Patterns of Objects in the Sky?

267

Step 4

Repeat steps 2 and 3 at noon and again in the afternoon. Compare the position of the sun and the shadows at the different times of day.

noon

afternoon

Step 5

Do the activity again another day. What patterns do you see?

Make a claim that answers your question.

_____

_____

_____

What is your evidence?

_____

Read, Write, Share! • Think about what you observed in the activity. Do you think the sun has always seemed to move this way?

✏️ Write to explain your ideas. Add details. Use new words you have learned.

_____

_____

_____

_____

Apply What You Know

Work with a partner. Make a model of the sun in the daytime sky. Use your model to explain the pattern of how the sun seems to move.

Lesson 1 • What Are Patterns of Objects in the Sky?

The Nighttime Sky

Explore Online

moon from Earth

moon close up

Night always follows day. On many nights you can see the moon in the sky. The **moon** is a large ball of rock that circles Earth. The moon seems to shine, but the moon does not give off its own light. The moon reflects light from the sun.

✏️ Write a fact about the moon.

_____

_____

_____

Explore Online

On a clear night, you can see many stars. Stars are balls of hot gases. These gases give off light. This light is what you see from Earth. Stars look tiny because they are far away. A telescope can help you see them better. It makes objects look bigger.

 Underline the sentence that tells why you can see stars.

Apply What You Know

Work with a group. Make a picture dictionary about the nighttime sky. List the objects in the nighttime sky. Draw a picture for each object. Write sentences to tell about it.

Lesson 1 • What Are Patterns of Objects in the Sky?

Patterns in the Nighttime Sky

Explore Online

The shape of the moon seems to change. These changes are called phases. **Phases** are the moon's pattern of light and darkness you see as the moon moves. The phases repeat each month.

Do the Math! • Draw an X on the phase of the moon that looks like a whole circle. Draw a box around the phases that look like half of a circle.

Explore Online

These are stars you can see during the summer.

These are stars you can see during the winter.

The sun is the only star you can see during the day. But the stars you see each night are not always the same. They change with the seasons.

Which sentences are facts about the patterns of the stars? Choose all correct answers.

Ⓐ The sun is the only star you can see during the day.

Ⓑ The stars at night in the winter are the same as the stars at night in the summer.

Ⓒ You can see different stars at different times of the year.

Apply What You Know

Evidence Notebook • Work with a group. Make a model of the phases of the moon. Use your model to tell about the pattern of phases of the moon. How does the moon seem to change? Use evidence to tell how you know. Record your answers in your Evidence Notebook.

Take It Further

People in Science & Engineering • Kalpana Chawla

Explore more online.
- Astronaut
- Space Technology

Explore Online

robotic arm

Kalpana Chawla was an astronaut and an engineer. She flew into space twice. Kalpana worked on the robotic arm of the space shuttle. She did experiments while in space.

Work in Space

Act like an astronaut. Pretend you are using a robotic arm. The arm is not moving. Which steps would you do to find a solution to the problem? Write 1, 2, 3, or 4 to order the steps.

_____ Test your solution.

_____ Decide if your solution works.

_____ Define the problem.

_____ Find a solution.

Lesson Check

Name _____

daytime

nighttime

Explore Online

Can You Explain It?

✏️ How do objects in the sky seem to change?

Be sure to
- Tell how objects seem to change in the sky.
- Describe the pattern of changes.

_____
_____
_____
_____
_____

Lesson 1 • What Are Patterns of Objects in the Sky?

Self Check

1. What causes the sun to seem to move in a pattern?

   Ⓐ Earth turns all the way around.

   Ⓑ The sun turns all the way around.

   Ⓒ The moon turns all the way around.

2. What time of day is it in each picture? Write the words from the box to label each picture.

   | night | late afternoon | noon |

   _____   _____   _____

3. How many times does the sun seem to rise in one week?

   Ⓐ 1

   Ⓑ 7

   Ⓒ 14

4. What is the moon?

   Ⓐ a large star that circles Earth

   Ⓑ a large ball of rock that circles Earth

   Ⓒ a large ball of rock that blocks light from the sun

5. What are the phases of the moon? Write the numbers to show the correct order. The first one has been done for you.

1 ____ ____ ____

6. What are patterns of objects in the sky? Choose all correct answers.

   Ⓐ The sun seems to move in the daytime sky.

   Ⓑ All stars appear in the daytime sky.

   Ⓒ The moon seems to change shape during the month.

Lesson 2
What Are Patterns of Daylight?

Patterns of daylight change throughout the year.

Explore First

Plan a Picnic Choose a season. Plan a picnic dinner for the season. How will the time the sun seems to set during that season affect your dinner? Record your ideas in your Evidence Notebook.

Changing Seasons

Explore Online

Observe the pattern of the seasons.

Can You Explain It?

✏️ You want to plant flowers in seasons with the most daylight. Which seasons would you choose?

_____

_____

Lesson 2 • What Are Patterns of Daylight?

The Seasons

Explore Online

spring

summer

winter

fall

A **season** is a time of year with a certain kind of weather. The four seasons are spring, summer, fall, and winter. The pattern of seasons repeats year after year.

Apply What You Know

Make a collage that shows a season. Label your collage with the season. Write sentences to tell about it. Share your collage with the class.

Spring and Summer

Explore Online

Spring comes after winter. The air gets warmer in most places. There are more hours of daylight than in winter. Spring days may be rainy. Warmer air and more daylight help plants begin to grow.

 Write a sentence that describes spring.

_____

_____

_____

Explore Online

Summer follows spring. The first day of summer has the most hours of daylight. Summer days are often hot and sunny. People dress to stay cool. Flowers and fruit grow on plants.

 Underline the sentence that describes summer weather.

Apply What You Know

Read, Write, Share! • Choose a season. Write facts to describe it. Have your partner guess the season. Take turns. Compare the facts. Did you find any patterns?

Fall and Winter

Fall comes after summer. There are fewer hours of daylight than in summer. Some animals store food for winter. The leaves of many trees change color and drop off. This is because there is less daylight.

 Write a sentence that describes fall.

_____

_____

_____

Explore Online

Winter follows fall. The first day of winter has the fewest hours of daylight. Winter is usually the coldest time of year. Some places get snow. People wear coats to keep warm. Some animals grow thick fur.

✏️ Write a sentence that describes winter.

_____

_____

_____

Do the Math! • This chart shows the seasons that some children like best.

How many more children chose summer than spring?

Ⓐ 5   Ⓑ 3   Ⓒ 4

Apply What You Know

Read, Write, Share • **Evidence Notebook** • Why do you think the weather changes throughout the year? Offer your opinion. Use evidence to support your opinion.

Lesson 2 • What Are Patterns of Daylight?

Patterns of Daylight

Explore Online

winter, 4:43 at night

spring, 7:13 at night

summer, 8:29 at night

fall, 6:57 at night

The amount of daylight changes from season to season. The sun rises and sets at different times during the year. This pattern repeats each year. Take a look at what time the sun sets in one place at the start of each season.

 Apply What You Know

Evidence Notebook • Work with a partner. Use evidence to explain the patterns of daylight during the year. Write your explanations in your Evidence Notebook.

Name_____

Hands-On Activity
Observe Patterns of Sunset

Explore Online

Materials
- a calendar
- crayons
- a computer
- drawing paper

Ask a Question

_____

Test and Record Data

Step 1

Identify the season and the date. Together, look up what time the sun will seem to set that day.

Step 2

Look up what time the sun will seem to set on a day in the next two seasons.

Lesson 2 • What Are Patterns of Daylight?

Step 3

Compare all the times you found. Record any patterns.

Make a claim that answers your question.

_____

_____

_____

_____

What is your evidence?

_____

_____

_____

_____

Take It Further

Careers in Science & Engineering • Circadian Biologist

Explore more online.
- Sarah Ballard
- The Midnight Sun

Explore Online

Circadian biologists study how seasons and daylight affect living things.

You may feel sleepier in fall and winter. Circadian biologists found out why. There is less daylight in fall and winter. This makes you feel sleepier.

Less daylight affects animals, too. They sense that it is time to get ready for winter.

Think about the people and animals in your home or community. How do the seasons affect them? How do they change?

✏️ Draw a picture to show what happens. Then write about it.

_____

_____

_____

Lesson Check

Name _____

Can You Explain It?

✏️ You want to plant flowers in seasons with the most daylight. Which seasons would you choose? Be sure to

- Tell how knowing patterns of daylight helped you decide which seasons to choose.

_____

_____

_____

Self Check

1. What is the order of the seasons? Write numbers to show the order. The first one has been done for you.

 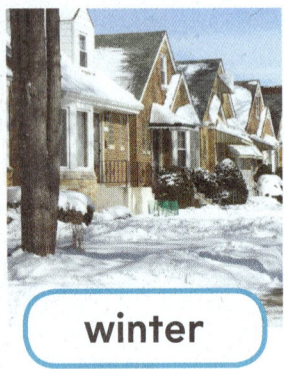  

spring — 1   winter — ____   fall — ____   summer — ____

2. This family is eating dinner at the same time in winter and in summer. Which is true about when the sun seems to set?

winter   summer

Ⓐ The sun seems to set earlier in summer.

Ⓑ The sun seems to set earlier in winter.

Ⓒ The sun seems to set at the same time in winter and in summer.

3. How often does the pattern of the seasons repeat?

   Ⓐ every year

   Ⓑ every week

   Ⓒ every month

4. If the sun seems to set at 7 o'clock on the first day of spring, when will it seem to set on the first day of summer?

   Ⓐ earlier than 7 o'clock

   Ⓑ later than 7 o'clock

   Ⓒ at the same time

5. Which is a pattern of daylight?

   Ⓐ The amount of daylight changes from day to day with the seasons.

   Ⓑ The amount of daylight changes from year to year.

   Ⓒ The amount of daylight never changes.

 # Unit Performance Task
Explore Short and Long Days

> **Materials**
> - two seedlings of the same kind
> - water
> - paper clips

STEPS

Step 1

Label one seedling **winter** and the other seedling **spring**. Measure the height of each seedling with paper clips. Record your observations.

Step 2

Place the seedlings in a sunny window. After one hour, put the **winter** seedling in a dark place. Leave the **spring** seedling in the sunny window.

Step 3

Put the **winter** seedling in the window for only one hour each day.

Step 4

Observe the seedlings for two weeks. Water the soil when it is dry. Measure and record the results every day.

Step 5

Use evidence to tell why a plant in spring might grow more than a plant in winter. Compare your results with the results of other classmates.

✓ Check

_____ I gave the **spring** seedling long days of sunlight.

_____ I gave the **winter** seedling short days of sunlight.

_____ I observed the seedlings for two weeks and recorded my observations every day.

_____ I explained why a plant in spring might grow more than a plant in winter.

_____ I compared my results to the results of my classmates.

Unit Review

Name _____

1. Which objects give off their own light? Choose all correct answers.
   Ⓐ moon
   Ⓑ sun
   Ⓒ star

2. When does the sun seem to rise?
   Ⓐ in the morning
   Ⓑ at noon
   Ⓒ at night

3. Look at the shadow in the picture. Where does the sun seem to be?
   Ⓐ low in the morning sky
   Ⓑ high in the noon sky
   Ⓒ low in the afternoon sky

4. Which pattern starts over again each day?
   Ⓐ The sun seems to move across the sky.
   Ⓑ The phases of the moon change.
   Ⓒ The seasons change.

5. What phase of the moon does the picture show?

   Ⓐ first-quarter moon
   Ⓑ full moon
   Ⓒ new moon

6. Look at the pictures. Which word describes each picture? Write a word from the word box.

   | fall   spring   summer   winter |

_____   _____   _____   _____

7. Alejandro wants to observe the pattern of the seasons from year to year. Which season will he observe always follows summer?

   Ⓐ spring
   Ⓑ fall
   Ⓒ winter

8. Which statements are true about fall?
   Choose all correct answers.
   Ⓐ There are fewer hours of daylight than summer.
   Ⓑ Some animals move to warmer places.
   Ⓒ Fall comes after summer.

9. Maya wants to observe patterns of daylight. Which day of the year will she observe has the most hours of daylight?
   Ⓐ the first day of winter
   Ⓑ the first day of spring
   Ⓒ the first day of summer

10. How is winter different from summer?
    Ⓐ Winter has fewer hours of daylight than summer.
    Ⓑ Winter has more hours of daylight than summer.
    Ⓒ Winter has the same number of hours of daylight as summer.

Interactive Glossary

This Interactive Glossary will help you learn how to spell and define a vocabulary term. The Glossary will give you the meaning of the term. It will also show you a picture to help you understand what the term means.

Where you see , write your own words or draw your own picture to help you remember what the term means.

behavior
A way an animal acts. (p. 192)

communicate
To share information. (p. 238)

G1

Interactive Glossary

design process

A plan with steps that helps people find good solutions. (p. 24)

engineer

A person who uses math and science to solve problems. (p. 10)

gills

Body parts that take in oxygen from water. (p. 165)

light
Energy that lets you see. (p. 52)

lungs
Body parts that take in oxygen from air. (p. 165)

mimic
To copy. (p. 115)

Interactive Glossary

moon

A large ball of rock that circles Earth. (p. 270)

offspring

The young of a plant or animal. (p. 128)

parent

A plant or animal that makes young like itself. (p. 128)

phases

The moon's pattern of light and darkness that you see as the moon moves. (p. 272)

pitch

How high or low a sound is. (p. 223)

problem

Something that needs to be fixed or made better. (p. 10)

Interactive Glossary

reflect

To bounce back from a surface. (p. 72)

season

A time of year with a certain kind of weather. (p. 282)

shadow

A dark place made when an object blocks light. (p. 88)

solution

Something that fixes a problem. (p. 10)

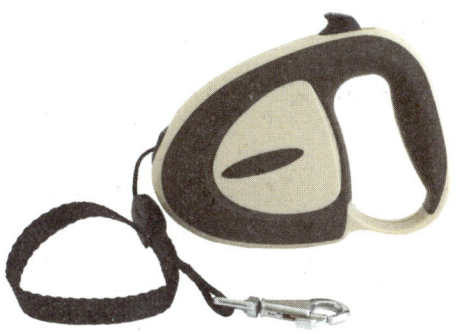

sound

A kind of energy you hear when something vibrates. (p. 220)

star

An object in the sky that gives off its own light. (p. 264)

Interactive Glossary

sun

The star closest to Earth. (p. 264)

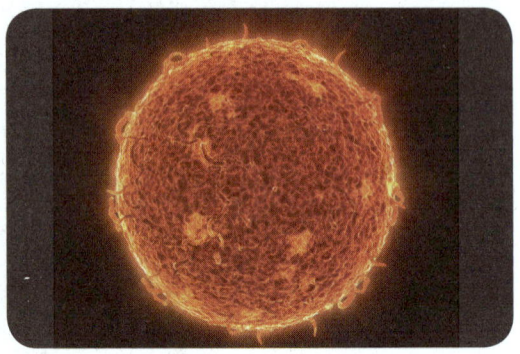

technology

What engineers make to meet needs and solve problems. (p. 13)

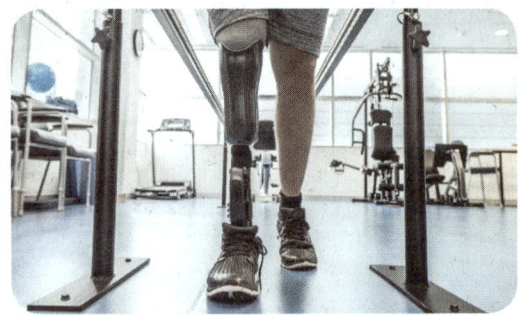

vibrate

To move quickly back and forth. (p. 220)

volume

How loud or soft a sound is. (p. 222)

Index

Abbott, Isabella, 121–122
adult
 animal, 172, 173, 174–175, 179, 180, 204, 210
 plants, 132
afternoon, 265–266, 268, 278
air, 165, 168
American Sign Language, 229
anteater, 179
Apply What You Know, 12, 14, 25, 26, 27, 28, 30, 54, 60, 71, 74, 87, 90, 111, 113, 116, 118, 129, 131, 133, 157, 159, 160, 161, 162, 166, 175, 179, 181, 184, 194, 196, 198, 221, 225, 226, 237, 240, 242, 264, 269, 271, 274, 282, 284, 287, 288
astronaut, 275–276

Bath, Patricia Dr., 91–92
bear, 161, 197, 205
behavior, 192, 195–196
bioengineer, 167–168.
 See also **engineer**
bird, 205, 208, 241
blubber, 171
body parts, 154, 158, 160, 161, 165–166, 176, 182, 188, 208
breathe, 165
butterfly, 158

cactus, 117
California quail, 239
California tree frog, 239
Camera Engineer, 77–78. *See also* **engineer**
Can You Explain It?, 9, 19, 51, 63, 83, 93, 127, 139, 173, 187, 191, 203, 219, 231, 235, 247, 263, 277, 281, 293
Can You Solve It?, 23, 35, 67, 79, 109, 123, 155, 169
carrots, 135
cell phone camera, 77
Chawla, Kalpana, 275
chicken, 180
Chinook salmon, 186
circadian biologist, 291
claws, 158, 161, 170
climbs, 159
communicate, 234–235, 238, 241, 245, 248, 249
Conway, Lynn, 33
cool, 117
coyote, 238, 240
cubs, 197, 205

danger, 158
dark, 51, 52, 57–60, 63, 65, 83. *See also* **darkness**
darkness, 51, 272
day, 273
daylight, 283, 285–286, 288, 291, 295
daytime, 263–265, 277, 280
design process, 24
 define a problem, 24, 25, 38
 plan and build, 26, 38
 test and improve, 27, 38
 redesign, 28, 39
 communicate, 29, 39
dogs, 182, 189
dolphin, 158
Do the Math!, 14, 30, 53, 74, 87, 113, 134, 161, 162, 184, 194, 225, 242, 272, 287

Earth, 264–265, 270

ears, 176, 185
ear bone, 185
early lamp, 62
Edison, Thomas, 61
electricity, 61–62
elephant, 166, 241
engineer, 8, 10–11, 13, 20–22, 162, 167, 229, 275
engineering, 1, 10, 162, 167
   packaging, 17
environment, 17, 121, 201
environmental scientist, 185
ethologist, 245–246
Explore First, 8, 22, 50, 66, 82, 108, 126, 154, 172, 190, 218, 234, 262, 280
eyes, 156, 157

fall, 281–282, 285, 291, 293, 294
feathers, 180
feet, 193
fish, 165, 166, 182, 185, 197
flies, 159
flippers, 158
food, 195–197, 204
frog, 161, 191
fruit, 110, 111
fur, 175, 180, 182, 188, 209, 286

gardens, 201–202
gases, 271
gecko, 162
gills, 165–166
great white shark, 156
grow, 128, 174
gulls, 195

Hands-On Activity, 15–16, 31–32, 55–56, 75–76, 85–86, 119–120, 135–136, 163–164, 177–178, 199–200, 227–228, 243–244, 267–268, 289–290
Hannigan, Robyn, 185
Hernandez-Rebollar, Jose, 229
heat, 264
hedgehog, 155, 169
hide, 193
high pitch, 223, 224, 239, 253
hot, 284

kangaroo, 158
katydid, 237
koala, 172

labs, 167
Language Development, 6–7, 48–49, 106–107, 152–153, 216–217, 260–261
leaf, 131, 146. *See also* **leaves**
leaves, 110–113, 132, 285. *See also* **leaf**
leopard, 197, 205
Lesson Check, 19, 35, 63, 79, 93, 123, 139, 169, 187, 203, 231, 247, 277, 293
light, 50–52, 54–55, 57, 59, 64–90, 93–95, 98–100, 112–113, 124, 264, 270–272
light bulb, 61–62
lily, 133
loud, 222, 224, 252
low pitch, 223–224, 239
lungs, 165

meerkats, 195
mimic, 115
Mizejewski, David, 201
moles, 157
moon, 264, 270, 272,

Index

279
morning, 265–266
mouse, 156
movie camera, 77

nature, 121
newborn, 174
night, 270–272, 273, 278, *See also* **nighttime**
nighttime, 262–263, 270, 272, 277. *See also* **night**
noon, 265–266, 278
nose, 156–157

objects, 255, 262–264, 279
offspring, 128
orangutan, 198
oxygen, 165

panda, 174–175
parent, 128, 174, 176, 181, 188, 189, 193, 197, 209, 239, 254
parent plants, 127, 130, 139–141, 146
parent trees, 128, 129, 131
pattern, 255, 262, 265, 272, 274,

278–281, 288, 295
penguin, 192
phases, 272, 279
pitch, 223
plant, 110–111, 114–117, 125–128, 130, 134, 144–145, 201–202
prairie dog, 156, 238, 247
problem, 10

quills, 160

rabbit, 192
raccoon, 180
Read, Write, Share!, 14, 34, 54, 62, 78, 92, 116, 122, 131, 138, 159, 166, 181, 186, 198, 225, 242, 246, 269, 284, 287
reflect, 72–73, 80, 100, 270
rhino, 176
roots, 110–111, 124

safe, 192–193
scales, 162, 180, 188
seasons, 273, 281–282, 287–288, 291–295
seed, 109–110, 125
Self Check, 20–21, 36–

37, 64–65, 80–81, 94–95, 124–125, 140–141, 170–171, 188–189, 204–205, 232–233, 248–249, 278–279, 294–295
senses, 156
shadow, 88–89, 93, 95, 99
shark, 162
shell, 160
skin, 166
soil scientist, 137–138
solution, 10
sky, 262–265, 270
snow, 286
soft, 222, 252
sound, 211, 213, 216, 218–223, 231–234, 236–239, 241, 248, 250, 252–254
space, 275–276
spines, 155
spring, 281–284, 287, 293–295
squirrel, 158, 170
star, 264, 271, 273–274
stem, 124
summer, 273, 281–285, 287, 293–295
sun, 264, 278, 288, 294
sunlight, 114, 146
swan, 173
swims, 159, 170
switches, 62

T

tadpole, 191
tail, 158
Take It Further
  Careers in Science & Engineering, 17–18, 167–168, 245–246, 291–292
  People in Science & Engineering, 33–34, 61–62, 77–78, 91–92, 121–122, 137–138, 185–186, 201–202, 229–230, 275–276
talons, 160
technology, 1, 8, 10, 20–21
teeth, 161
telescope, 271
tongue, 161
tree, 108
trunk, 176
tulips, 132, 141
turtle, 170

U

Unit Performance Task, 38–39, 96–97, 142–143, 206–207, 250–251, 296–297
Unit Project, 3–5, 45–47, 103–105, 149–151, 213–215, 257–259
Unit Review, 40–42, 98–100, 144–146, 208–210, 252–254, 298–300

V

vibrate, 220, 232, 236–237, 252, 254
volume, 222

W

water, 110
whiskers, 156–157
wings, 158
winter, 273, 281–283, 285–286, 291, 293–294
wires, 62

Y

You Solve It, 1, 43, 101, 147, 211, 255
young, 239
  animal, 172–173, 176, 180–181, 187–190, 192, 195, 197–198, 203–205, 209–210
  plants, 127, 130, 139–141, 146. *See also* **plants**
  trees, 128–129. *See also* **trees**

Z

zebra, 165